THE
MYSTERY
OF
DOGGERLAND

"Graham Phillips has made a powerful case for advanced prediluvian civilization in Europe. In fact, the sunken kingdom of Doggerland, only recently discovered at the bottom of the North Sea, resembles in many ways the lost world called Atlantis by Plato. Phillips does a great job of showing the connections between the mythic megalithic culture we have dreamed about for many centuries and one we had long forgotten but which may be the true homeland of the British people. A wonderful and intriguing read."

J. DOUGLAS KENYON, AUTHOR OF *GHOSTS OF ATLANTIS: HOW THE ECHOES OF LOST CIVILIZATIONS INFLUENCE OUR MODERN WORLD*

"Graham Phillips's well-researched, well-written book neatly places a number of missing pieces in the puzzle of the Orkney megalithic tradition and the broader ancient region of Doggerland. He presents these in context with a range of informative viewpoints on prediluvian cultures including Atlantis, Mu, and Lemuria."

LAIRD SCRANTON, AUTHOR OF *THE MYSTERY OF SKARA BRAE, SACRED SYMBOLS OF THE DOGON,* AND *POINT OF ORIGIN*

THE
MYSTERY
OF
DOGGERLAND

ATLANTIS IN THE NORTH SEA

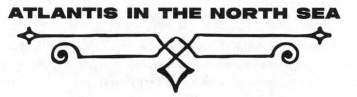

GRAHAM PHILLIPS

PHOTOGRAPHY BY
DEBORAH CARTWRIGHT

Bear & Company
Rochester, Vermont

Bear & Company
One Park Street
Rochester, Vermont 05767
www.BearandCompanyBooks.com

Bear & Company is a division of Inner Traditions International

Cataloging-in-Publication Data for this title is available from the Library of Congress

ISBN 978-1-59143-423-8 (print)
ISBN 978-1-59143-424-5 (ebook)

Printed and bound in the United States by Versa Press, Inc.

10 9 8 7 6 5 4 3 2 1

Text design and layout by Kenleigh Manseau
This book was typeset in Garamond Premier Pro with News Gothic Std, Gill Sans
MT Pro, and Gotham Narrow used as display typefaces
Photographs by Deborah Cartwright, Earthquest Photography,
earthquestphotography.com

To send correspondence to the author of this book, mail a first-class letter to the
author c/o Inner Traditions • Bear & Company, One Park Street, Rochester, VT
05767, and we will forward the communication, or contact the author directly at
grahamphillips.net.

In loving memory of Storm Constantine

Contents

Acknowledgments

The author would like to thank the following people for their invaluable help: Deborah Cartwright for the wonderful photography; Yvan Cartwright for his fantastic IT support; Jodi Russell for extra research material; my researchers Helena Brooks and Jade Attridge; Sally Evans, Dave Moore, and Claire Silverman in helping with translations; and Jon Graham, Patricia Rydle, Kelly Bowen, Kayla Toher, Will Solomon, and all the team at Inner Traditions.

Global Warning

·····························

What History Has to Teach Us

In one way or another, the coronavirus pandemic has adversely affected nearly everyone on Earth, shattering our way of life, devastating the world economy, causing untold suffering, and leaving millions dead. Covid-19 is frightening enough, but there is a far more perilous and long-term threat to human life: climate change. If unchecked, global warming will almost certainly result in the submergence of some of the Earth's largest metropolitan conurbations; entire nations will be pounded by overwhelming mega-hurricanes, gargantuan tornados, and their coasts thrashed by huge tsunamis; vast wildfires will rage out of control, consuming farms, forests, and cities; an intolerable number of animal and plant species will become extinct; and famine on a worldwide scale will decimate humanity. Furthermore, deadly viruses, far worse than Covid-19, may well be released from melting ice, and diseases, against which we have no resistance, could all but exterminate humanity. How do we know? Not only through scientific projections, but because it has all happened before. What follows is the terrifying true story of what occurred when the planet critically warmed between 7000 and 4000 BCE. In this book we will be examining the terrible catastrophes that devastated cultures millennia before the rise of ancient Egypt, when an increase in global temperatures by just a few degrees led to the complete annihilation of some of the world's first civilizations.

1

A Forgotten Civilization

·····································

People of the North Sea

We begin by examining evidence of extreme flooding events that occurred in ancient times on a worldwide scale, starting with a recent find off the northernmost coast of the British Isles. Here, as we shall see, extraordinary archaeological discoveries have revealed how the consequences of prehistoric climate change all but wiped out a sophisticated culture years in advance of its time. An ancient stone circle, earthworks, an artificial mound, and fallen monoliths, all located on the seabed of the North Sea, offer dramatic evidence for the dreadful carnage that occurred the last time the Earth heated up.

Around 3000 BCE, the inhabitants of Great Britain and Ireland transformed rapidly into the so-called Megalithic culture, the builders of Stonehenge and hundreds of other stone circles unique to the British Isles.* Across these islands monumental complexes were erected, consisting of huge stone circles surrounded by ringed ditches and embankments (called henges, from which Stonehenge gets its name), accompanied by

---

*Just to save confusion, the word *Britain* refers to both the individual countries of England and Wales; Great Britain is England, Wales, and Scotland; the United Kingdom [UK] is Great Britain and Northern Ireland; and the British Isles is Great Britain and all Ireland. It should be noted that, for obvious reasons, the people of the Irish Republic prefer the term *West European Isles.* With apologies to the Irish, I shall be using the term *British Isles,* as it is the one with which most readers will be familiar.

massive artificial mounds, stone avenues, and freestanding monoliths. Such complexes were scattered throughout the countryside with smaller stone circles in between, often linked by alignments of solitary monoliths covering many miles. Yet from this era there are no written records, as writing did not come to the British Isles until the Roman invasion in the first century CE. As with so much concerning the Megalithic culture, its origins are shrouded in mystery.

Before continuing, a few terms should be clarified. The word *megalith*, which we shall often use to refer to the standing stones erected during the period, comes from the ancient Greek *megas* ("large") and *lithos* ("stone"). The term *Megalithic*, with a capital *M*, we will use to refer to the culture of the British Isles that created them, and *megalithic*, not capitalized, will apply to the monuments built by that culture, regardless of whether they are made of stone.

It was once thought that the Megalithic culture began in the south of England, where Stonehenge is situated, before moving north, perhaps originating with migrants from northern France where there are many ancient standing stones. However, there is no evidence of stone circles and their accompanying monuments specifically like those in the British Isles in France or anywhere else in continental Europe. Since the advent of scientific dating techniques, it is now known that the oldest stone circles are those in the northern British Isles, implying that the practice began there and *then* moved south. The revised conjecture was that it began around five millennia ago on the Orkney Islands off the north coast of Scotland where the oldest datable stone circle was found.

Despite this, it seems highly unlikely that the Megalithic culture originated even there. Surprisingly advanced for the time, the Megalithic culture appeared on the Orkney Islands *abruptly*—virtually overnight in archaeological terms—with a complex societal structure, mastery of building techniques, sophisticated ceramics, and an astonishing knowledge of medicine *already* established, implying that it must

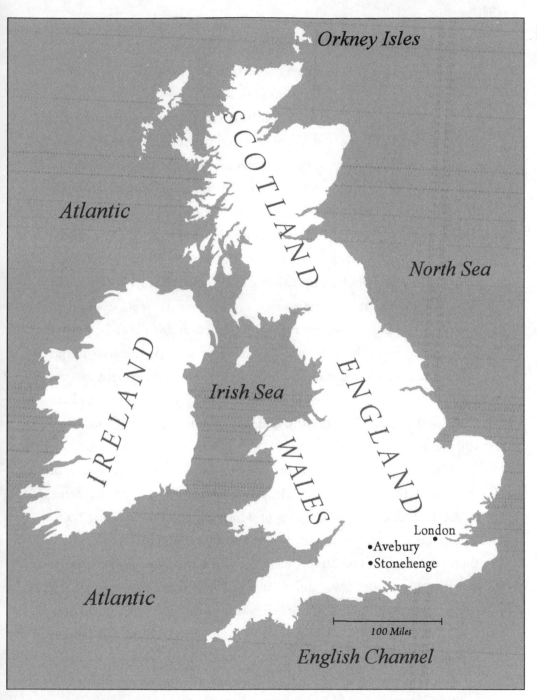

Fig. 1.1. The British Isles, showing the locations of Avebury, Stonehenge, and the Orkney Islands.

surely have started and developed elsewhere. However, modern experts have long been baffled as to where this might have been. Nowhere in mainland Europe or Scandinavia was there anything remotely similar. So where *did* the Megalithic culture originate?

Stonehenge is the Megalithic culture's most famous creation. Yet the monument we see today, constructed around 2500 BCE, is far from the oldest stone circle in the British Isles. That *was* the Stones of Stenness, some 700 miles to the north. The Stenness stone circle stands in isolated, windswept heathland on an island called Mainland, the largest of the Orkney Islands, which lie some 10 miles off the northern tip of Scotland. It now consists of four stones, up to 15 feet high, standing in a semicircle, with three smaller monoliths lying flat inside the arrangement. As with many stone circles, over the years stones have been toppled and broken up for building materials or smashed apart by vandals. From the radiocarbon dating of organic material found beneath the stones still standing, the circle seems to have been erected around 3100 BCE and, from telltale signs in the soil, it appears to have once consisted of 12 monoliths, equally spaced in a circle of just over 100 feet in diameter.

Mainland Isle additionally boasts one of the largest stone circles in the British Isles. The Ring of Brodgar is some 340 feet in diameter, originally consisting of 60 stones of which 27 remain, standing up to 15 feet high. It was surrounded by a 400-foot-diameter circular ditch about 10 feet deep and 30 feet wide with an outer embankment, much of which has eroded away due to its exposure to the relentless North Atlantic weather. Some 450 feet southwest of the stone circle is an artificial hillock called Salt Knowe, a 130-foot-wide, 20-foot-high mound thought to have been built at the same time.

In 2011, in the Bay of Firth off the eastern coast of Mainland Isle, marine archaeologists carrying out a routine underwater survey using remote sensing and seismic profiling (radar and sonar) discovered a submerged circular embankment. Working in an area known as North Doggerland, the archaeologists came upon what was clearly an artificial construction with an inner ditch about 450 feet in diameter. On closer examination, within the ring there seemed to be the remains of a stone circle: six fallen monoliths about 15 feet long lying on the seabed, their regular shape revealing them also to be artificial creations. When their locations in relation to one another were taken into consideration, they appeared to have been the remains of a stone circle about 350 feet in diameter that may have originally consisted of some 50 to 60 monoliths. Additionally, about 450 feet southwest of the circle there appeared to be the remains of an artificial hillock, 130 feet in diameter and some 10 feet high. All this suggested the archaeologists had discovered a very similar monument to the Ring of Brodgar. The size, number, and height of the stones, the surrounding ditch and embankment, its diameter, and the nearby artificial hillock, were almost identical.[1]

This was indeed a fascinating discovery, but apart from the fact that it was underwater it seemed nothing unique. The remains of many Brodgar-like, large stone circles exist throughout the British Isles, such as at Avebury, 17 miles north of Stonehenge. These huge stone circles, with their surrounding earthworks, are referred to as megalithic complexes, of which there were dozens created throughout the British Isles. As these megalithic complexes date from the most active period of stone circle building, between around 3000 and 2500 BCE, archaeologists assumed that the sunken circle dated from that time and was submerged when water levels rose. But all that changed in 2019 when marine archaeologists were able to dive the site. (It had taken some years to get financial backing for the project.) Everyone was astonished when dating revealed the monument to be at least 6,000 years old.[2] This date of approximately 4000 BCE, perhaps earlier, made the construction around 1,000 years older than the Stones of Stenness, the earliest known stone circle at that time. To put this into context, this was 1,000 years before the first kings of Egypt, and one and a half millennia older than the pyramids of Giza. And the sunken complex was as sophisticated as the megalithic complexes throughout the rest of the British Isles that were not built until after 3000 BCE.

There could be no doubt that, well before stone circles were erected anywhere else in what is now the British Isles, an advanced megalithic complex was created on dry land that once existed around the Orkney Islands and is today known as North Doggerland. So, was it in some long-ago sunken realm to the north of Scotland that the Megalithic culture originated? The monumental complex on the seabed of the Bay of Firth is just one piece in an extraordinary jigsaw puzzle of historical and archaeological clues revealing that a sophisticated civilization, hundreds of years older than anything from ancient Egypt, Mesopotamia, or India—previously thought to have been the locations of the world's first true civilizations—once existed on what had once been dry land to the northeast of the Orkney Islands. An ancient culture with prehistoric technology years beyond its time. As we shall see, it had the most advanced ceramic and weaving techniques anywhere in the world, created huge monuments, invented the sauna, and had medical knowledge unknown until the modern age. It seems that once this previously unknown civilization disappeared beneath the sea, aspects of its knowledge were adopted by the people of the British Isles. In other words, remnants of this lost civilization appear to have established what we now call the Megalithic culture. We shall be examining all this later. For now, let us examine just *how* such a civilization might have sunk beneath the waves.

It is all to do with the Ice Age—or rather its end. The last Ice Age began around 110,000 years ago, reaching its peak around 20,000 BCE when the average world temperature was some 5 degrees Celsius (10 degrees Fahrenheit) lower than today. That might not sound like much, but it enabled the polar ice caps to grow to an astonishing size, rendering large areas of the Earth uninhabitable. And with so much

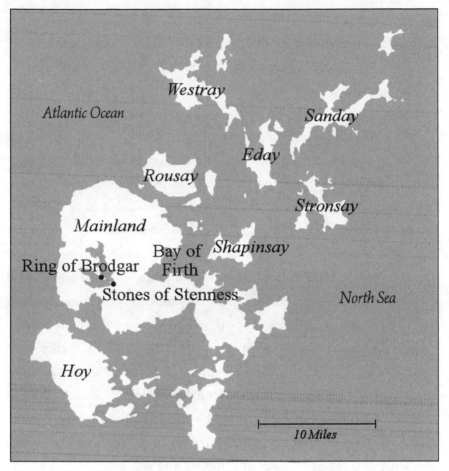

Fig. 1.2. The Orkney Islands, showing the locations of the Ring of Brodgar, the Stones of Stenness, and the Bay of Firth.

water tied up in ice, there was less rainfall worldwide, and even in the tropics prolonged droughts spelled disaster for plants, animals, and human beings. The northern polar ice cap, over half a mile thick, spread south beyond the Great Lakes in North America and to southern Britain in Europe. By then, so much of the world's water was tied up in ice that global sea levels were an astonishing 400 feet lower than they are today. Scientists can determine prehistoric sea levels by examining the remains of coastal marine vegetation and fossilized coral from around the world. Fauna and flora that live in shallow waters die as sea levels rise, and so finding their remains in strata of underwater silt enables dating. Around 20,000 years ago temperatures began to rise, possibly caused by a slight shift in the Earth's orbit around the sun. Ice melted, and the glaciers and vast ice sheets began to retreat. By 14,000 years ago sea levels had risen by approximately 140 feet.

By 10,000 BCE the emergence of new land previously under ice had led to significant migrations of human populations and the beginning of farming and village settlements—as opposed to the previous hunter-gatherer way of life. This was the so-called early Neolithic era of our existence. (The word *Neolithic* means new or late Stone Age, and the term *Stone Age* refers to the manufacture of stone implements—although most of them were probably made from wood and bone.) By then, due to the continually melting ice, global sea levels had risen to about 190 feet lower than today, and over the following three millennia the waters kept rising until by 7000 BCE they were some 100 feet lower than modern times. This brings us to an era of human history known as the mid-Neolithic, when advances in the cultivation of crops and domestication of animals had led to larger settlements. Within another thousand years, in many parts of the world, humanity had entered an age of ceramics and sophisticated brickmaking, and the first settlements of more than 1,000 inhabitants had been established.[3] (Pottery and mud bricks had been made before this time although their use had been limited.) Around 4000 BCE the so-called late Neolithic age began, characterized by the smelting of soft metals such as gold, silver, and copper for jewelry, high-status ornaments, and ritual objects—although, in terms of tools and utensils, the world was still in the Stone Age. By now ice melting had stabilized and sea levels were only around 12 feet lower than today. Which brings us back to North Doggerland, and back to the megalithic complex in the Bay of Firth. As it lies about 12 feet below the present sea level, it must have begun to submerge about 4000 BCE.

As it had to have been built some time before it began to submerge, the underwater megalithic complex on North Doggerland in the Bay of Firth must be at least 6,000 years old. And the civilization that built it had to be older than that for its people to have developed a culture and the skills necessary to create it. Whoever its builders were, they appear to be a lost civilization that existed on once dry land east of the Orkney Islands during the mid-Neolithic. Lost, maybe, but far from forgotten. It is not only that the late Neolithic culture of the British Isles might have developed from its remnants but, remarkably, that it may still have been remembered by the ancient peoples of the British Isles generations after the Neolithic age.

In fact, millennia after the first megalithic monuments were erected in the British Isles, legends persisted concerning a prosperous land that once existed to the north of Scotland, which had been lost to the sea in the remote past. The oldest written records concerning Britain were made by Greek explorers at the time of Alexander the Great, around 325 BCE. The native Britons of the time, the Iron Age Celts (who first arrived from mainland Europe around 700 BCE), told them of a lost realm that once existed to the north of their country: a sunken island they called Tu-lay. It was said to have been an island paradise that sank beneath the waves when the inhabitants angered their sea god. It was from here, the Celts maintained, that the builders of the first stone circles originated. Indeed, legends of a sunken land to the north of Britain still survived to be recorded by foreign visitors to the British Isles many centuries later, particularly in Ireland where much ancient mythology was recorded by Christian missionaries who first arrived during the fifth century CE. According to a collection of ancient Irish myths and legends brought together into one volume during the Middle Ages as *The Book of Invasions,* long ago certain chosen people on a remote island were warned by the gods of a coming flood and sailed away to avoid the catastrophe.[4] (*The Book of*

Invasions was not committed to writing in its present form until the eleventh century, but the story was preserved in the fifth-century *Book of Druimm Snechta*. This no longer exists in its entirety, though much of it is quoted in other medieval collections of ancient Irish prose and poetry.[5]) Might the discovery by marine archaeologists of the sunken megalithic monument in the North Sea be evidence that this lost land of Celtic mythology was more than mere legend?

One account in *The Book of Invasions* concerns a man called Fionn mac Cumhaill (pronounced Finn McCool), an Irishman who is said to have voyaged first to the southwest coast of Scotland and then, after sailing three more days around the west and north coasts of Scotland, reached what seems to be John o' Groats, mainland Great Britain's northernmost point. From there he sailed north to discover an island referred to as *tír an ghealltanais,* or "land of promise." Once more we are told that this is where the first stone circle builders originated. The same island is also the subject of a further tale in *The Book of Invasions,* an account called *The Story of Cessair.* Cessair (pronounced Kah-seer) is a holy woman or mystic who experiences a vision that her native island will be overwhelmed by a great flood. She instructs her faithful followers to build ships to find a new place to live. Hearing of Fionn's homeland of Ireland, it is to there that Cessair and her followers migrate. (Interestingly, later Irish missionaries Christianized Cessair as the daughter of the biblical Noah.)

Most of these Irish accounts fail to name the sunken island. The oldest surviving Irish work that does name it was written by the eighth-century monk Dicuil in his work *Liber de Mensura Orbis Terrae* (Concerning the measurement of the world), which is based on a geographical text called *The Measuring* compiled on behalf of the Byzantine emperor Theodosius II around CE 435. In Dicuil's work the mysterious island is referred to as Tu-lay—the very name of the lost land related to earlier Greek and Roman explorers.[6] Indeed, there are numerous classical references to it under various renderings such as Tyle, Tile, Thule, and Thoule. The oldest surviving text to specifically refer to Tu-lay is found in *On the Ocean* by the Greek explorer Pytheas. Composed around 320 BCE, Pytheas's work was compiled shortly after Alexander the Great was leading his army to conquer the known world, when geography became a subject of crucial interest. Just how big *was* the world? If the Greeks and Macedonians (who made up Alexander's army) were to extend their conquests beyond the Mediterranean and the east, should they turn to the north? Having heard tales of a mysterious, bounteous land somewhere to the north of Scotland—probably the same or similar Celtic legends as those heard by the Christian missionaries many centuries later—Pytheas traveled as far north as he could, reaching the northern tip of Scotland. Evidently, the intrepid explorer does not appear to have heard the part about Tu-lay having long ago sunk beneath the sea. When he sailed to where Tu-lay was said to have been, he found nothing. All he discovered was a group of small, sparsely populated islands just to the south of Tu-lay's supposed location, probably the Orkney Islands.[7]

Having heard the legends of the Britons, other writers from the ancient Mediterranean world also refer to Tu-lay: the first-century BCE Greek astronomer Geminus of Rhodes in his *Introduction to the Phenomena;*[8] the Greek historian Strabo in his *Geography,* written around 30 CE;[9] the Egyptian explorer Dionysius Periegetes in his *The Position of the Habitable World,* written around 120 CE;[10] and the fourth-century Roman writer Rufius Festus Avienus in his *The Sea Coast.*[11] They all agree that Tu-lay was said to have been a fertile island situated somewhere to the north of Great Britain.

In CE 77, a degree of confusion was added when the Roman writer Pliny the Elder wrote his *Natural History,* in which he muddles the references to Tu-lay with historic voyages of some of his contemporaries, placing the lost land within the Arctic Circle, seemingly identifying it as Iceland.[12] However, nothing previously written about the mysterious island places it anywhere near so far north. Unfortunately, some later authors followed Pliny's erroneous lead: using his misinterpretation as their source, they placed Tu-lay far away from the British Isles. For instance, in the early 500s CE the Greek historian Procopius of Caesarea identified Tu-lay as a part of southern Sweden, over 700 miles to the east of Scotland.[13] Yet in the first century, the Roman historian Tacitus, writing around CE 98, describes how the Romans circumnavigated Great Britain, learning from the native inhabitants the widely held myth that Tu-lay had existed just north of the Orkney Islands. Tacitus was writing on good authority concerning the mythology of the Britons. The reference is found in his *On the Life and Character of Julius Agricola,* which concerns his father-in-law who had been Roman governor of Britain.[14] And the fourth-century Roman linguist and commentator Maurus Servius Honoratus, who made an in-depth study of Celtic mythology, learned directly from the Britons that Tu-lay was thought to have been close to the Orkneys.[15]

In conclusion, early classical visitors to the British Isles seem to have heard the legend of Tu-lay, but confusion arose as to whether it still existed or had sunk beneath the waves. Although later writers began placing its location farther and farther away from the British Isles, the earlier authors all agreed that it was somewhere just north of the Orkney Islands. Interestingly, the oldest surviving map to depict Tu-lay, the *Carta Marina* (made in 1539 by the Swedish cartographer Olaus Magnus), shows it directly above the Orkney Islands. He quotes as his source the legends of the Scots. Whether or not such an island ever historically existed is a question we shall return to later. Suffice to say at present, it was clearly a part of Celtic mythology that a fertile and prosperous island called Tu-lay (or something similar) had existed just to the north of the Orkney Islands off the north coast of Scotland. If the legend of Tu-lay originated with a real land, as the discovery of the megalithic complex in the Bay of Firth might suggest, how could such a legend have survived to be related to the Greeks and Romans over three and a half millennia after the land was finally submerged? And by a people who had no native form of writing?

Although the British Isles was home to a succession of foreign migrants between 2600 BCE and the arrival of the first Greeks in the fourth century BCE, the influence of Megalithic culture persisted throughout this entire period. The conventional Megalithic age, when the largest and greatest number of megalithic monuments were built, was between around 3100 and 1200 BCE and involved three separate cultures: the original Neolithic, the Beaker people, and the Wessex culture. However, stone circles continued to be used and repaired, and new ones erected, by further migrants, the early Celts—the Bronze Age Urnfield and Iron Age Hallstatt cultures—right up until the Roman invasion of the first century CE. Astonishingly, whatever purpose the megalithic monuments served, they seem to have appealed to a succession of completely different cultures.

The first to build stone circles in the British Isles were the late Neolithic people who used simple stone, bone, and wooden tools. Although they had probably inhabited these islands from around 4000 BCE (see chapter 10), from the construction of the first stone circles, around 3000 BCE, they can be referred to as the early Megalithic culture. Then, around 2600 BCE, a mass influx of foreigners into the British Isles came from what is now the Netherlands, driven by rising sea levels flooding their low-lying homeland. (The sea had only risen by a few feet over the previous four centuries, but that was enough to submerge vital farming land.) No one knows what the migrants called themselves, but archaeologists have termed them the Beaker people, after a distinctive type of bell-shaped pottery vessel, or "beaker," found in their graves. However, their arrival was clearly not an invasion. No archaeological evidence has been found that the Beaker people and the native population engaged in fighting to any discernible extent. No defenses were erected around settlements, and no human remains have been unearthed exhibiting the kinds of injuries sustained in battle. On the contrary, the two peoples seem to have lived and worked harmoniously together, while at the same time retaining their cultural identities—as indicated by, for example, the fact that the newcomers' burial mounds contained their distinctive beakers, whereas the contemporary indigenous population continued to bury their dead without funerary goods.[16]

Around 2000 BCE there was a new influx of people into Britain, this time from what is now Belgium. Known as the Wessex culture, after the region of south-central England where their remains were first identified, they brought with them the beginnings of the British Bronze Age. (Bronze is made by mixing copper with a small amount of tin, forming an alloy that is much harder and more useful than either metal alone.) However, unlike the first civilizations of the Middle East and India, they had not developed the technology to make the alloy in the quantities necessary to revolutionize daily life. Bronze was a rare and valuable commodity, and its use was generally restricted to the making of ritual objects. Although bronze axes, arrowheads, and even swords have been found dating from the late Neolithic period in the British Isles, these seem to have been made for a privileged few, probably the tribal leaders. For the most part, implements continued to be Stone Age items made from flint, bone, and wood. As with the arrival of the Beaker people over five hundred years earlier, there is no evidence of fighting between the Wessex culture and the pre-existing population. Just like the Beaker people before them, the Wessex culture seems to have embraced the stone circle tradition, as evidenced by excavations at megalithic complexes created after their arrival— though, once again, they retained their own religious customs, such as the burial of their dead in cistvaens, simple rectangular boxes dug into the earth and lined with flat stone slabs with capstones placed over their tops.[17]

The Beaker people and Wessex culture migrations seem to have been driven by rising sea levels that affected their homelands in the low-lying coastal areas of the Netherlands and Belgium. The migration of a new people, however, originally from an area that now includes Austria and Germany, seems to have been triggered by the sudden onset of a period of colder weather. Until around 1200 BCE the British climate was warmer than it is today, more like we would now find in southern France or northern California. But then, quite quickly, the overall climate changed from what is known as the Subboreal to the Subatlantic climatic age, and temperatures dropped significantly. This has been determined by the remains of vegetation unearthed by archaeologists from the relevant levels of human occupation, showing the extinction of certain warm-weather flora and a marked increase in the kind of plants and trees that favor colder conditions.[18] Various theories have been proposed for this climatic change, involving shifting ocean currents, volcanism, and an alteration in the sun's activity. Whatever the cause, not only the British Isles but also other parts Europe grew colder, leading to dramatic consequences. In Austria and Germany, a cultural revolution was already taking place. This was the Germanic Bronze Age, when the alloy began to be produced in sufficient quantities to make a real difference to daily life. (The Bronze Age started at different times throughout the world, beginning around 3300 BCE in Mesopotamia, or modern Iraq.) Bronze tools, such as more efficient spades, axes, knives, and farming implements, replaced more fragile Stone Age ones. On the one hand this was fortunate, because the longer, colder winters meant that producing enough food was becoming ever more problematic. But with harsher conditions came protectionism. To safeguard their precious resources, settlements began to be fortified, and the new bronze tools made it easier and faster to build much bigger earthen structures, such as defensive ditches and embankments, and to work lumber into wooden stockades. Around 1200 BCE, fortified hilltop settlements began to replace the open communities of the lowlands. Generally referred to as hillforts, these new communities consisted of a cluster of dwellings on a relatively flat-topped hill around which a ditch was dug, together with an internal embankment surmounted by timber ramparts and a fortified gatehouse to guard the entrance. Inevitably, this siege mentality, together with the new bronze technology, led to the development of weapons of war, such as swords, battle-axes, daggers, and metal-tipped arrows and spears.[19] A completely new kind of warrior culture was being born, a people the Greeks later referred to as the Keltoi. Today we know them as the Celts. As their dead were cremated and their ashes placed in pottery urns buried in fields, archaeologists refer to them as the Urnfield culture. Yet despite the turmoil created by these warlike people in mainland Europe, when they crossed the English Channel to settle in Britain these newcomers not only brought with them the true Bronze Age to the British Isles, but became as obsessed as their predecessors with using, repairing, and building stone circles—and the Megalithic age continued.[20]

By around 700 BCE the last wave of pre-Roman people arrived in Britain. For a hundred years or so, the Urnfield culture in continental Europe had been transformed by the Iron Age, when iron replaced bronze for the making of most common utensils, tools, and weapons. The melting point of iron is just over 1,500 degrees Celsius (2,732 degrees Fahrenheit), around 1,300 degrees Celsius higher than tin and nearly 500 degrees Celsius higher than copper, the primary components of bronze. Iron's industrial production therefore occurred much later than bronze. It is generally thought to have begun in the Hittite Empire, centered on what is now Turkey around 3,000 years ago, although this is still a matter of scholarly debate. One way or another, by 800 BCE the Iron Age had reached Austria where it rapidly changed the entire nature of the Urnfield culture and initiated a new period of Celtic expansion.[21] It was for these reasons that once the Urnfield culture in Austria and Germany had mastered the

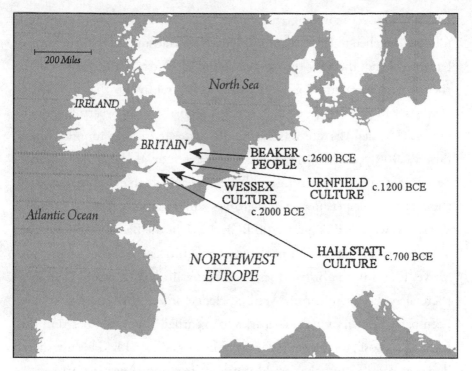

Fig. 1.3. Prehistoric migrations from mainland Europe to the British Isles.

secrets of iron production, they quickly assumed control of much of central and northwestern Europe. This new Celtic phase is known as the Hallstatt culture, named after a site near Salzburg in Austria close to the modern border with Germany, where a huge cemetery of the period was excavated during the nineteenth century.[22] From around 700 BCE, when they first arrived in Britain, until the Roman invasion of the first century CE, the Hallstatt people were the dominant culture here, yet archaeology and the writings of the Greeks and Romans reveal that they too continued to revere Megalithic sites and the ancient stone circles. In fact, they even seem to have embraced the Megalithic priesthood or its senior caste.[23] (See chapter 10.)

So, it is quite possible, with the adoption of at least some aspects of the Megalithic culture by these successive waves of migrants, that the myths and legends of the original Neolithic inhabitants of the British

Isles were passed on in oral tradition. Many ancient sites have legends and folklore attached to them that must have been transmitted for generations by word of mouth. Near the town of Mold in North Wales, for instance, there stands an earthen mound called Bryn yr Ellyllon that for centuries was said to be haunted by a woman reported to be wearing "golden armor."[24] When the site was eventually excavated it was found to contain a 4,000-year-old skeleton wearing a ceremonial chest-and-shoulder adornment made from solid gold. Because of its shape and size, it is thought that the person buried there was a high-ranking woman, possibly a priestess who died around 1900 BCE. Now in the British Museum, the so-called Mold Cape is one of the most magnificent pieces of prehistoric art yet found in the British Isles. The figure in "golden armor" had lain there at peace for millennia, yet knowledge of her burial seems to have been passed down over the centuries to eventually be remembered in the form of a ghost story. Even if the account of her burial had been written down at some point, that could not have been until writing arrived in Britain with the Romans. At the very least, knowledge of the burial must have been conveyed by word of mouth for around 2,000 years.[25]

Another example of such long-lasting oral tradition is associated with the Cheesewring, an unusual rock formation on Bodmin Moor in Cornwall in Southwest England. Folklore related how travelers who became lost on the moors were guided to safety by an immortal Druid who dwelled in the vicinity, who would also offer them sustenance from a golden cup.[26] When a nearby burial mound called Rillaton Barrow was eventually excavated the remains of a high-status individual, thought to have been an early Bronze Age priest, were discovered along with grave goods including a pure gold cup, probably used for ceremonial purposes. The mound had remained undisturbed for over 3,500 years, so once again it seems that folk memory of the person buried there with a gold goblet was transmitted from generation to generation by word of mouth until it transformed into the legend of the helpful Druid.

Such long-lived oral traditions have survived intact for centuries throughout the world, some for very much longer than those of the British Isles. When Europeans first arrived in what is now Oregon in the western United States in the early nineteenth century, they were told tales by the Klamath people who lived around Crater Lake about how the lake was formed. They were told that the lake, which the Klamath called Giiwas, had long ago been created in a great battle between powerful spirits when a mountain had stood there. The day skies turned to night and fire rained down from above until the mountain collapsed, leaving a huge hole in the ground that eventually filled with water to become Crater Lake.[27] Modern geological research has shown that the lake was indeed formed in much the way the Klamath described. It had once been a volcano, destroyed by a massive, explosive eruption. Fiery pumice would have rained down over a vast area of the surrounding countryside, and a dark volcanic ash cloud would have blotted out the sun for miles around. All that remained of the volcano was what is known as a volcanic caldera that filled with rainwater to become Crater Lake. But how could the Klamath people have known this? Geology has revealed that the event had been the only such eruption in Oregon in the last million years—and it happened around 5700 BCE, some seven and a half thousand years before the Europeans heard the Klamath story.[28] The Klamath had no writing before the Europeans arrived, so the account must have been handed down verbally for over an astonishing seven millennia, or perhaps as pictorial representations drawn on skins or rocks. These are just a few examples demonstrating how societies without writing could indeed pass down traditions, myths, legends, and religious notions, unchanged for as long as the Megalithic culture endured in pre-Roman Britain.

The ancient peoples of the British Isles maintained an oral tradition that the Megalithic, stone-circle building culture that they embraced had begun on a long-lost land to the north of the Orkney Islands, until that land ultimately sank beneath the waves. The archaeological discovery in the Bay of Firth tends to confirm that there may well have been such a place. Today we call it Doggerland, but it's hard to say what its inhabitants may have called it. At the very least, a megalithic complex was built on now-sunken land off the Orkney Islands centuries before identical monuments were created elsewhere in the British Isles. We shall return later to examine archaeological evidence for a lost civilization north of the British Isles; for now, however, we need to appreciate that its possible fate was just a small part of a dreadful, ongoing cataclysm that affected the entire world.

2

First Cities and the Legend of Atlantis

Possible Locations and Catastrophes

Many of our ancestors had abandoned a nomadic hunter-gatherer existence to settle in small villages of some hundred or so people from the early Neolithic era (the period of early farming) around 10,000 BCE. Around 7000 BCE, during the mid-Neolithic, in various parts of the world human settlements—often referred to by archaeologists as the *first cities* (for convenience, a term I shall be using in this book)—became much larger, with up to 1,000 inhabitants, and within a thousand years some had populations of many more. Their ruins have been excavated throughout the world: Plovdiv in Bulgaria, Erbil Citadel in Iraq, Tell Sabi Abyad in Syria, Jiahu in China, Mehrgarh in Pakistan, Belovode in Serbia, Huaca Prieta in Peru, Monte Verde in Chile, Huaca Prieta in Peru, Yarim Tepe in Iran, Çatalhöyük in Turkey, and Jericho in Palestine (fig. 2.1, p. 23). These early cities were, however, nowhere near as elaborate as the ancient cities with which we are most familiar today, such as those of Greece and Rome. The earliest of those kinds of cities, with tens of thousands of inhabitants, large dwellings, street planning, municipal buildings, and an urban hierarchy, such as those of Sumer in southern Iraq, ancient Egypt, and the Indus Valley civilization of Pakistan and northwest India, were not built until after 3300 BCE during the Bronze Age.[1]

Although there were regional variations, the cities of the mid-Neolithic were remarkably similar considering they are found across the globe. A good example is the thoroughly excavated city of Jericho, astonishingly still a town today, which gives us a general idea of the appearance and development of these cities during the early Neolithic period. Now within the Palestinian West Bank territory, the ruins of ancient Jericho are found on a hill called Tel es-Sultan, about a mile north of the modern town. Occupied from around 9600 BCE, the original settlement consisted of about seventy circular dwellings, each about 16 feet across, made from clay and straw bricks, and roofed with hard, dried, mud-smeared scrub. By around 7000 BCE, Jericho had grown to become one of the so-called first cities of the mid-Neolithic: a 430,000 square-foot settlement of a few hundred dwellings housing as many as 3,000 people, surrounded by an oval, mudbrick wall over 12 feet high and 6 feet wide, some half a mile in circumference. The inhabitants of this early city farmed pulses, wheat, and barley, and had domesticated sheep and goats, although they had no oxen, horses, or beasts of burden. Within a couple of centuries, by 6800 BCE, the population had grown to an estimated 5,000, and buildings had become much larger, rectangular mudbrick structures, each consisting of several rooms clustered around a central courtyard. Walls were whitewashed; internal floors were made from lime, which even today still contain the impressions of reed and rush mats; the courtyard floor was made from hardened clay. Among the ruins, archaeologists have uncovered fragments of portable vessels made from lime plaster, bowls and dishes carved from limestone, stone spindle whorls and loom weights used in the making of wool and cloth garments, and human statuettes fashioned from plaster, as well as life-size clay figurines depicting various animals.[2]

Although the use of horses as a means of transport, oxen as draft animals, and the invention of the wheel did not occur anywhere until

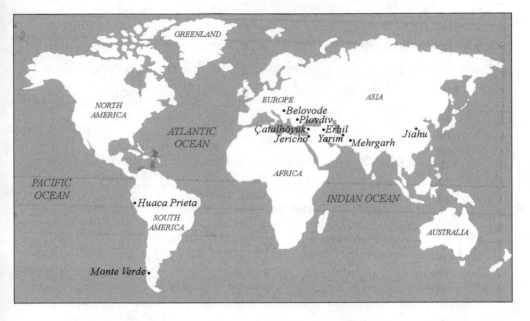

Fig. 2.1. Some of the world's earliest mid-Neolithic cities.

the late fourth millennium BCE, excavations have revealed that some of the first cities had made cultural and technical innovations far in advance of anything once thought possible for the time. For a start, some of these settlements were truly huge for the period. For instance, Çatalhöyük in Turkey, founded about 7000 BCE, had a population of around ten thousand.[3] At Jiahu in China, 14 miles north of the modern city of Wuyang in Henan Province, a city covering approximately 600,000 square feet existed by around the same time. Not only had the Jiahu people developed an early form of writing by carving into bones and tortoise shells three and a half thousand years before writing was thought to have been invented in Mesopotamia, they also created the world's oldest known musical instruments in the form of flutes carved from the wing bones of cranes.[4] At Tell Sabi Abyad in Syria, pottery was already being mass produced as early as 6700 BCE,[5] and by 6000 BCE, the people of Yarim Tepe in Iraq even had sophisticated updraft kilns—as opposed to firing pottery in simple pits dug into the ground—enabling them to create much higher temperatures that allowed glazing. This was three millennia before such kilns were invented in Egypt.[6] At two early cities, Pločnik and Belovode in Serbia, archaeologists have even found evidence of copper smelting dating from as early as 5300 BCE, two thousand years before the Bronze Age.[7]

Most settlements during this time, however, were still small farming communities, as they had been since the start of the Neolithic. Early cities, such as Jericho, Çatalhöyük, and Mehrgarh, were the exceptions. The relative sophistication and prevalence of these so-called first cities has only been appreciated in recent times, and they still lack an accepted generic term to describe them. They are often referred to merely as *mid-Neolithic settlements,* which can lead to confusion as this term also refers to the more modest farming villages of the time. So, apart from the term *first cities,* I shall also be using the word *urbian*—from the Latin meaning "relating to an urban environment"—to distinguish them from the other types of mid-Neolithic settlements, and additionally to differentiate them from the later, more complex cities such as those in Sumer, Egypt, and the Indus Valley.

Most of these mid-Neolithic urbian cities were built on high ground, but there would undoubtedly have been many more such settlements established in coastal locations to act as fishing and trading communities. Simple boats capable of sea travel are known to have existed well before these first cities were built; the oldest boat yet discovered in its entirety, preserved in a peat bog in the Netherlands, is a dugout canoe made from a hollowed tree trunk around 8000 BCE. However, dating from two thousand years earlier, a rock carving in Azerbaijan depicts a reed boat paddled by twenty people, while impressions found preserved in excavated soil in many parts of the world have revealed that from this time large rafts made from wood, bamboo, and other floating material were able to carry heavy goods or as many as thirty passengers for considerable distances. But seafaring goes back much, much earlier. Archaeological evidence that Australia had been populated as early as 60,000 years ago means that, even with lower sea levels, humans had to have crossed many hundreds of miles of open water millennia before the first cities were built.[8] The early coastal settlements, or harbor towns, from where sea voyages were made, either to islands or along the coast, would certainly have been submerged as sea levels rose (as discussed in chapter 1) by about 90 feet between 7000 and 4000 BCE. But, if the surviving hilltop citadels are any indication of their construction, coastal cities were mainly concentrations of simple mudbrick or wooden dwellings rather than stone-built structures, meaning that all evidence of them will have been obliterated by millennia beneath the waves. Nevertheless, memory of some of these early harbor settlements may have been preserved in oral tradition before being committed to writing. Could they be the very places referred to in ancient mythology as having perished during age-old prehistoric floods?

Legends concerning primeval lands lost to the sea are in no way unique to Britain. The most famous comes from the Greek world—the legend of Atlantis. The oldest surviving reference to Atlantis is found in the works of the Greek philosopher Plato, writing around 360 BCE. According to him, thousands of years before his time this mighty island kingdom, located somewhere in the Atlantic Ocean, finally sank beneath the waves in a single day, during a catastrophic flood, after its inhabitants angered the sea god Poseidon. At face value Plato's Atlantis seems pure invention. As described in his dialogues *Timaeus* and *Critias,* a magnificent palace stood at the heart of the Greek-style buildings of Atlantis's capital. The entire city was surrounded by three huge circular moats, crossed by many bridges, and linked by canals, with a further channel connecting them to the sea so that great ships could sail into the fortified harbor. The metropolis was enclosed by three massive stone walls covered in brass, tin, and something Plato calls orichalcum, possibly the ancient name for platinum, each entrance protected by gigantic gates and towers guarded night and day.[9] Such a mammoth undertaking as Plato describes would not have been possible in Plato's day, let alone millennia earlier as he claims. In fact, the vast expense would have prevented even the later Romans, with their innovative building techniques and the invention of concrete, from attempting to construct such an extravagant city. According to Plato, the island was submerged some 9,000 years before his time. This would be approximately 11,350 BCE, at the end of the Ice Age, when humans throughout the world were still living a hunter-gatherer existence in small nomadic family groups—well before permanent villages, let alone the early cities, were built. Yet Plato maintains that the people of Atlantis, the Ατλάντες—Atlantes—often transcribed as "Atlanteans," sailed the seas in great war galleys (historically not invented until the eighth century BCE) to conquer Libya and Egypt, before being defeated by the Athenians, even though Athens was not founded until 508 BCE.[10]

Over the years, there have been many theories regarding sunken islands that might have given rise to the story of Atlantis—far too many to be examined here. Two of them, however, do deserve serious consideration. The sunken islands of these theories were not flooded anywhere near as long ago as Plato maintained, but they might nonetheless have started the legend.

The first is the dramatic destruction of the volcanic island of Thera (modern Santorini) in the Aegean Sea, home to the Greek Islands. Between 3,500 and 3,300 years ago a series of volcanic eruptions destroyed much of the island, resulting in catastrophic tsunamis (also known as tidal waves) that pulverized the coastal towns of the Minoan civilization on nearby islands, including Crete where the Minoans had their capital. As this once mighty seafaring civilization went into decline and ultimately ceased to exist during this period, it is believed that the destruction of many of its ships and harbors resulting from these tsunamis led to its demise. Accordingly, various Aegean islands occupied by the Minoans that had been hit by the Thera tsunamis have been proposed as inspiring the Atlantis legend.[11]

The second concerns possible evidence of ruins off the coasts of Cuba and the Bahamas, which might imply urban development, even a formidable civilization, as long ago as 1500 BCE, and perhaps much earlier. The mythologies of the indigenous peoples of Central America talk of a lost civilization in the Caribbean, a place the Aztecs called Aztlan—possibly the origin of the name Atlantis.[12] That the peoples of the Mediterranean could have known of this Central American legend would mean that they, or alternatively the ancient Mesoamericans, crossed the Atlantic at least two thousand years before Columbus. The jury is still out on whether such voyages were possible at the time.

However, if transatlantic voyages were accomplished before Plato's day, it is possible that tales of Aztlan could have been confused with the tradition of a sunken island closer to the Mediterranean that may have given rise to the story of Atlantis. Alternatively, accounts of the dramatic demise of the Minoans, the most advanced civilization in the Mediterranean of their time, could have contributed to the Atlantis legend. However, for the purposes of this book we need to determine where exactly the ancient Greeks considered Atlantis to be—based on *their* surviving works. Although it clearly wasn't Doggerland, it might well have sunk at about the same time, giving us some idea of what might have occurred to the island I have referred to as the Atlantis in the North Sea.

Scholars generally agree that Plato's account of the highly developed culture of Atlantis was a philosophical or political allegory, never intended to be taken as historical fact. Nevertheless, it is quite possible that the author did base the story of the sunken island on existing mythology, even if he invented its wondrous civilization and implausible size. Plato says that Atlantis "was an island greater in extent than Libya and Asia Minor" combined.[13] The ancient land of Libya, which included what is now northern Libya, Algeria, and much of Tunisia, covered approximately 12,000,000 square miles, while Asia Minor—what is now much of Turkey south of the Bosporus—was around 300,000 square miles. So, according to Plato, Atlantis covered at least 12.3 million square miles—the size of India. From any geological or scientific perspective, there has never been such a landmass in the Atlantic Ocean, at least not since the age of the dinosaurs. Such embellishments aside, it is possible that Atlantis, minus its magnificent city and of a more feasible size, was a real island. Plato is known to have borrowed some of his allegories from older traditions—for instance, the story of King Gyges and his magical ring, found in his work *Republic*.[14] Gyges of Lydia, in modern-day Turkey, was a historical figure who reigned between 687 and 652 BCE, and the legend concerning his ring of invisibility was related to Plato's older brother Glaucon when he visited Lydia around 400 BCE. Regarding Atlantis, Plato claims to have heard of the island from a now-lost work of the Athenian statesman Solon, who had learned of it in Egypt around 585 BCE.

According to Plato, Atlantis was overwhelmed by an enormous flood before sinking forever beneath the sea. This is not so unbelievable as it sounds. First, we should determine where exactly Atlantis was thought to have been. We are told that, as determined from the location of Greece, it had been somewhere beyond the Pillars of Hercules—what we now call the Strait of Gibraltar at the far western end of the Mediterranean—meaning that it was assumed to have been somewhere in the Atlantic Ocean. In his *Timaeus,* Plato writes about a supposed struggle between the Atlantes and the peoples of the Mediterranean countries as "the war which was said to have taken place between all those who dwelt outside the Pillars of Heracles [the Atlantes] and those who dwelt within them [including the Lydians, Greeks, and Egyptians]."[15]

Over the years writers have speculated on many possible locations for a historical Atlantis way out in the Atlantic Ocean. However, satellite surveys have shown that the waters of the Atlantic have been far too deep—an average of over 13,000 feet—for millions of years, too long to have been the location of an island that sank during the period of human existence. But that is not necessarily the case for the continental shelves of Europe, Africa, Greenland, Antarctica, and the Americas.

This is still a huge area. So, what else can we infer from Plato regarding the legendary island's supposed location? Interestingly, nowhere does he imply that Atlantis was far out in the ocean, merely that it was somewhere west of the Strait of Gibraltar. More likely, if the island did exist, it was relatively close to the Mediterranean civilizations of Plato's time, quite possibly off the western coast of southern Europe, or the coast of northwest Africa. In fact, in his *Timaeus*, Plato has his character Critias specifically declare that Atlantis "was an island situated in front of the mouth of which you Greeks call the Pillars of Heracles."[16] The *mouth* of the Pillars of Heracles, what we now call the Strait of Gibraltar, was and still is the sea between Tangier in northwest Morocco and Tarifa in southern Spain. Plato's words, "in front of the mouth," imply that it was just to the west of this location. But was this the northern, southern, or central mouth? Well, Plato's words clearly favor the southern promontory off the coast of Morocco in northwest Africa, inferred from Atlantis's connection with the legendary figure Atlas.

In his *Critias*, Plato says that Atlas had been the first king of Atlantis: "[Poseidon] begat ten male children, dividing the island of Atlantis into ten portions . . . the eldest, who was king, he named Atlas. And from him the island and the sea were named [Atlantis and Atlantic] . . ."[17] This is a vital clue as to where Atlantis was thought to have been, as Atlas was associated with Morocco. Stretching to some 50 miles offshore, the waters here are only about 70 feet deep, and in its relatively shallow depths marine surveys have revealed that many ancient islands did indeed succumb to rising sea levels during the period when the world's first cities flourished, between around 7000 and 4000 BCE. Even today, tradition holds that Atlas was the first king of Mauretania—modern northern Morocco—the notion coming from the works of classical authors who firmly connect him with that area. According to the ancient Greek poet Hesiod, in his *Theogony* (Genealogy of the Gods) written around 700 BCE, when Atlas was punished by Zeus for rebelling against the gods he was condemned to hold up the heavens* at the ends of the Earth in the land of his daughters, the Hesperides: "And Atlas, standing at the borders of the earth before the clear-voiced Hesperides, upholds the wide heavens."[18] According to various classical writers the land of the Hesperides was in an area the Greeks referred to as Ampelusia, now Cap Spartel, a promontory including modern Tangier, which the Greeks believed was the last land in the west before the Atlantic. For example, in his *Natural History,* completed around CE 77, the Roman writer Pliny the Elder tells us that the Greeks considered the land of the Hesperides to be "beyond the Pillars of Hercules, now in Tingi [modern Tangier]."[19] Tangier was, and still is, a major port city on the Cap Spartel in what had been northwest Mauretania. And the Roman poet Ovid relates the ancient Greek legend that Atlas had once ruled Mauretania. In his *Metamorphoses,* written around 2,000 years ago, he tells us that here Perseus used the head of Medusa to turn Atlas into a mountain at the extreme western end of what became known as the Atlas Mountains, in a range now called the Er-Rif, which bounded Tangier to the east, south, and west.[20] That Atlas had been

---

*Note that it is the skies, and not the Earth, that Atlas supports on his shoulders. The common depiction of Atlas holding up the world was a later Roman notion dating from the second century CE. The word *atlas,* a collection of maps, is known by that name from a sixteenth-century tradition of featuring this Roman depiction on the cover of such volumes.

king of both Atlantis *and* Mauretania would imply that the two lands were closely related. (Remember, Atlas was supposedly the *first* king of Atlantis, well before his successors began their conquests.) In fact, it seems that the peoples of these lands were believed to have been one and the same. Astonishingly, Herodotus, a Greek historian who wrote around 450 BCE, almost a century before Plato, tells us precisely that. Although not mentioning Atlantis itself, he refers to the people who lived at the far western end of what he calls "the Ridge" as the Atlantes—the people of Atlantis.[21] The Ridge was what is now known as the Tell Atlas Mountains, the western end of which is the Er-Rif range. Evidentially, Mauretania and Atlantis were thought to have been two parts of the same kingdom. So, the best bet for the location that Plato, Solon, or their sources had in mind for Atlantis would be somewhere off the northwest coast of Morocco, not far from Tangier.

Modern marine surveys of the Tangier coast have revealed that there was indeed an island just a few miles out to sea. Until about 3 miles offshore the sea off northwest Tangier is less than 70 feet deep, before dropping off sharply to about 1,000 feet. Then, a further 9 miles out to sea, there is a submerged embankment known as the Majuán Bank, which rises to just 50 feet below sea level. This was once a sizable island referred to by geologists as Majuán Isle. Judging by modern radar, sonar, and satellite surveys, it is estimated that around 7000 BCE Majuán Isle was about 6 miles long and 3 miles wide, rising to some 50 feet above sea level, and only 9 miles off the coast of Mauretania as it existed at the time. Over the next thousand years sea levels rose, slowly but surely, by about 50 feet, until the entire island was finally submerged around 6000 BCE.[22] If Majuán Isle was the island of Atlantis, then the likelihood that it was home to an advanced civilization is remote, to say the least, but around 7000 BCE an early city-state, such as its contemporaries Jiahu,

Jericho, and Çatalhöyük, may well have existed here, and originated the Atlantis legend. Unfortunately, however, if it was anything like the mid-Neolithic first cities of the time, then nothing is likely to remain today. Even if there is some evidence still to be examined, the dangerous waters where the Mediterranean meets the Atlantic make marine archaeology far too hazardous for the foreseeable future.

If Atlantis was indeed the island of Majuán, then it would have sunk steadily by about 5 feet a century, which is less than three-quarters of an inch a year: plenty of time for the island to have been gradually abandoned. But Plato suggests Atlantis was engulfed in a single day. He talks about an overwhelming flood shaking the earth itself.

A natural cataclysm that would fit such a description is a tsunami. Tsunamis caused by coastal or undersea earthquakes can be truly devastating. In 2011, a magnitude 9.0 earthquake 70 miles off the coast of Tohoku triggered a powerful tsunami that devastated parts of eastern

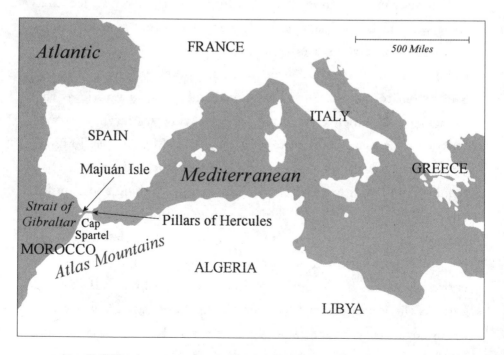

Fig. 2.2. The location of Majuán Isle, possibly the historical Atlantis.

Japan with a wave that reached a height of 130 feet and traveled over 6 miles inland. It devoured almost everything in its path, killing around 20,000 people and leaving many thousands more with life-changing injuries. A quarter of a million people had their homes and workplaces destroyed. In addition, the tsunami triggered multiple explosions and the terrifying meltdown of the Fukushima Nuclear Power Plant. More powerful waves, known as teletsunamis, are so powerful that they can travel thousands of miles. For example, a magnitude 9.5 earthquake on the coast of Chile in 1960 sent a 200-mile-an-hour tsunami right across the Pacific to hit New Zealand, Australia, the Philippines, and even Japan—10,000 miles away. The most horrific teletsunami of modern times was the so-called Boxing Day Tsunami of 2004. An earthquake off the west coast of northern Sumatra sent a series of massive tsunamis across the Indian Ocean to pummel the coasts of Sri Lanka and India with waves up to 100 feet high. In all, the tsunamis killed an estimated 227,898 people in fourteen countries all around the Indian Ocean. But the power of such teletsunamis is nothing compared to the might of the megatsunamis that happened a few thousand years ago as the polar ice caps melted.

Geological surveys have revealed that gigantic megatsunamis occurred as glaciers retreated after the Ice Age. Streams from melting glaciers had carried trillions of tons of sediment to the edge of the continental shelves of Greenland, Europe, Siberia, and North America, and triggers, such as earthquakes, could result in massive underwater landslides, sending huge tidal waves right across the widest of oceans.

Based on the examination of the continental shelf in the Norwegian Sea, and from the carbon dating of organic material retrieved from sedimentary deposits, a series of such enormous landslides, called the Storegga Slides, are known to have occurred on the coast of Norway. In the most recent, around 6200 BCE, the collapse of an astonishing

840 cubic miles of debris—an equivalent volume to an area the size of Ireland to a depth of 112 feet—caused a massive megatsunami to cross 3,500 miles of the North Atlantic at an estimated 400 miles an hour to thrash the eastern seaboard of North America with a wave over 100 feet high. And the carbon dating of ancient plant material deposited by the tsunami reveals that the wave traveled at least 50 miles inland.[23] If this happened today, cities like New York, Boston, and Philadelphia would be destroyed, and millions would perish.

Another such landslide off the coast of southeast Greenland occurred some years earlier, around 6500 BCE, sending a smaller, but still devastating, megatsunami in a southeasterly direction across the North Atlantic, traveling at hundreds of miles an hour and hammering the coasts of southwestern Europe and northwest Africa with a wave about 30 feet high. At this time Majuán Isle, off the coast of

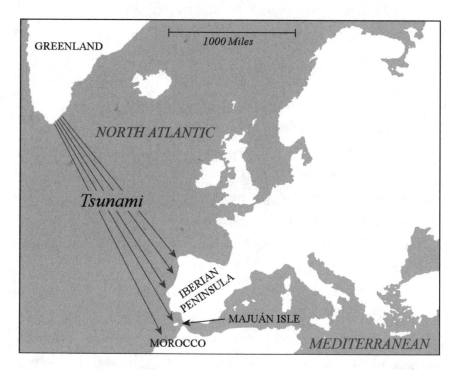

Fig. 2.3. Direction of the Greenland Slide megatsunami around 6500 BCE.

Morocco, would still have been a habitable island about 4 miles long and 2 miles wide, rising to some 25 feet above sea level.[24] If it were the island behind the story of Atlantis, it would have been completely drowned by the 30-foot Greenland Slide tsunami in much the way Plato describes. Indeed, geological surveys of northern Morocco show that the area suffered the effects of just such a megatsunami at exactly this time. Evidence of what is known as high-energy marine flooding around Tangier was found, in the form of boulders, shells, and sand, among datable organic deposits, about a mile inland from the current coastline. That would have been over 10 miles inland from the coast of 6500 BCE, indicating a tsunami of about 30 feet high.[25]

None of this supports Plato's description of a sophisticated Greek-style culture with construction techniques millennia in advance of the time, certainly not the modern notions of a technological civilization way ahead of our own. Neither is it evidence of a lost land the size of India. But it does show that an island, perhaps sustaining an early city like those mentioned above, did exist exactly where Plato and his contemporaries had in mind. And it appears that it was completely inundated by a gigantic wave in a single day as Plato describes. Once the tsunami passed, the sea levels would have dropped to what they had been, and Majuán Isle would have survived until it ultimately succumbed to rising sea levels over the following centuries. Its inhabitants, however, would have been totally wiped out. It is possible that later seafarers found the island empty and, staggered by the pulverized remains of its settlements, initiated what would become the legend of Atlantis.

Whether Majuán Isle was indeed the legendary island of Atlantis, the mighty megatsunami that crashed into it around 6500 BCE graphically demonstrates just how the melting ice caused by the rising temperatures following the Ice Age could have resulted in catastrophic landslide tsunamis that destroyed some of the world's earliest cities— including any at North Doggerland. The Greenland Slide most likely wiped out many other low-lying cities on the western coastlines of Europe and Africa, and there were probably many other such periodic megatsunamis yet to be identified. But megatsunamis are unlikely to have wiped out *all* the early coastal cities thought to have existed in prehistoric times. Nonetheless, most of them were to ultimately perish as sea levels rose. And this is what may have given rise to legends not only of sunken islands but of entire lost continents.

3

Lost Continents

·····························

Debunking the Theories of Mu and Lemuria

Just as the Atlantic has Atlantis, various researchers have advocated a sunken civilization in the Pacific: the lost land of Mu, ultimately to be regarded as an entire continent. The original concept, first proposed by the British antiquarian and archaeologist Augustus Le Plongeon in the late nineteenth century, was somewhat different. Based on his interpretation of findings among the ruins and texts of the ancient Maya, he considered Mu to have been another name for Atlantis, which he concluded had not only been the source of early Mediterranean civilization but also the origin of ancient Mesoamerican culture.[1]

In 1873 Le Plongeon and his wife, the photographer Alice Dixon, traveled to Yucatán in southern Mexico to investigate the Maya's principal ruins. The Maya had established a complex society throughout much of Central America by at least 3,000 years ago, its empire eventually incorporating southeast Mexico, Guatemala, Belize, western Honduras, and El Salvador. From its heyday it left behind marvelous stone-built cities with highly sophisticated architectural constructions, such as stepped pyramids, temples, governmental buildings, and palaces, all resplendent with statues, carvings, and elaborate glyphs.[2]

The civilization developed the first form of writing in the Americas, revealing not only their history and religious beliefs but also their accomplishments in mathematics and astronomy.

It was obvious to antiquarians of the nineteenth century that the ancient Maya were as advanced as many civilizations in the Old World, and some, such as Augustus and Alice, were convinced that there was a link between the Maya and the ancient Egyptians. For a start, both civilizations erected pyramids, both had accomplished mathematicians, architects, and astronomers, and both used symbols to convey meaning in written language. In fact, as in Egypt, during the Le Plongeons' time Mayan writing was even referred to as hieroglyphics. When they visited Mexico in 1873, Augustus and Alice were searching for evidence of just how the two cultures, almost 8,000 miles apart and separated by a vast ocean, could have been related. It was soon apparent from frescos, carvings, and artworks that, like the ancient Egyptians, the Maya did not seem to have possessed boats capable of crossing the Atlantic. Perhaps the occasional vessel might, with extreme good luck, have succeeded, but certainly no voyages occurred on a scale for one culture to have influenced the other to any extent. Nevertheless, the couple were still convinced there was a relationship, and they began seeking another possibility: an intermediary culture. Surely, they reasoned, some third civilization with the necessary seagoing vessels and navigational skills had linked Egypt and Central America. And before long Augustus was certain he had found evidence of just that.[3]

Shortly after their arrival in Mexico, while in the city of Mérida, the capital of Yucatán state, Alice contracted yellow fever and spent months recuperating. It was at this time that Augustus familiarized himself with the work of Charles Étienne Brasseur de Bourbourg, a nineteenth-century French Catholic priest and amateur archaeologist who in the mid-1800s had made a translation of the so-called Troano Codex, a pre-Columbian manuscript consisting of Mayan characters painted on a long strip of paper made from pulped tree bark. Translating ancient Mayan was somewhat easier than translating Egyptian hieroglyphics in the early nineteenth century. That had to wait for the deciphering of an ancient Egyptian text accompanied by a copy in a known language: the Rosetta Stone, carved with the same text in both Egyptian hieroglyphs and a known language, ancient Greek. In Mexico, however, ancient Mayan was not a dead language. When the Spanish first arrived during the early 1500s, although the Mayan civilization

Fig. 3.1. Central America and the extent of the Maya civilization.

had been eclipsed by the Aztecs of central Mexico, the Maya people still survived as an independent enclave in the Yucatán Peninsula in the southeast of the country. Even today, there are over six million descendants of the Maya who still speak various dialects of their ancestors' tongue. In the manuscript Brasseur found repeated glyphs that he determined were pronounced *Mu*—the name of a land that had supposedly long ago been submerged by the sea.[4] Brasseur had assumed the story to be nothing more than myth, but to Le Plongeon it was just what he was looking for. Surely, he thought, this was a reference to Plato's Atlantis. Perhaps the third civilization that linked the Maya and the ancient Egyptians was Plato's famous sunken island. What if both the Maya and the ancient Egyptians were descendants of the Atlanteans? Alice concurred with her husband, and on her recovery, they set off into the rain forest to find further evidence of their Mu-Atlantis hypothesis.[5] When we appreciate just how spectacular were the Mayan ruins they discovered, it is quite understandable how, in the days before modern archaeology, the Le Plongeons became so convinced that the Maya were the remnants of an earlier lost civilization.

One ancient Mayan site visited and excavated by the Le Plongeons was Chichen Itza, some 75 miles east of Mérida, which at the time was completely covered by jungle vegetation. Excavations began in earnest in 1875 with permission and labor provided by the Mexican government. When cleared, Chichen Itza turned out to be a typical Mayan city. Indeed, it provides us with an excellent example of just how advanced the civilization really was. Its dense cluster of large stone structures cover an area of about 2 square miles, although smaller residential dwellings would have made the full city of around 35,000 people much larger. Many of the city center buildings were in an astonishing state of preservation, considering that they had been abandoned for centuries to the encroachment of the rain forest. The reason was that the stonework was set against a concrete substructure and held together by cement. In fact, the Maya developed such building materials even before the Romans, the only other ancient civilization known to have utilized cement and concrete to such an extent.[6]

Typical of Mayan cities, the heart of Chichen Itza was both a religious and administrative center, divided into two separate compounds encircled by low stone walls. The entire complex had been artificially leveled, and its buildings were connected by a dense network of paved walkways. The northern compound is dominated by the Kukulkan Pyramid, named after a Mayan god depicted as a feathered serpent. It consists of nine 8-foot-high square terraces of diminishing dimensions, the base terrace measuring 180 feet across, with stairways in the middle of all four sides. On the upper platform stands a rectangular temple building, about 20 feet high, making the entire structure some 100 feet tall. When the Le Plongeons first arrived in 1875 the top of this structure rose above the forest canopy; at the time, this was one of the only indications that an ancient city was hidden among the vines and creepers of the jungle's lofty, dense trees.[7]

To the northwest of the Kukulkan Pyramid is the Jaguar Temple, named after reliefs depicting these large cats. It is basically two temples, one above the other. Set on top of a steep 30-foot pyramidal base is a 15-foot-high rectangular upper temple reached by four external flights of steps, one on each side, bordered by balustrades decorated with images of the feathered serpent. This upper temple entrance is flanked by squat, freestanding pillars in the shape of the same deity, Kukulkan, while the interior walls and ceiling were once covered with paintings showing scenes of both battles and domestic life. Attached to the outside of the pyramidal base at ground level, on the opposite side to the entrance to the upper temple, the lower temple entrance is a portico supported by two square columns, between which is a stone throne in the form of a jaguar. The interior of the lower temple is covered with intricate carvings in bas-relief showing Mayan warriors wearing elaborate feather headdresses and a figure sitting on a jaguar throne like the one at the entrance. Adjoining the Jaguar Temple is the Great Ball Court. Measuring 550 by 230 feet, it was where the Mesoamerican game of Ōllamaliztli was played, in which the players struck a heavy rubber ball with their hips in the attempt to score goals through a stone ring set high on a wall. The game had important ritual associations, with formal tournaments held as ceremonial events. However, it was also a popular pastime played by men, women, and children. In all, thirteen ball courts have been identified at Chichen Itza.[8]

To the southeast of the Kukulkan Pyramid is another temple called the Temple of the Warriors. It consists of a truncated four-stepped pyramid, some 40 feet high and 130 feet wide, fronted by rows of about 100 round and square pillars. Carved with scenes depicting warriors, after which the structure is named, these columns would once have supported a roof forming a large, covered entrance lobby. From here a wide flight of steps ascends the front of the base to arrive at a stone sculpture depicting a reclining figure holding a bowl. Called a *chac-mool,* it is a common motif in pre-Columbian Mesoamerican art, and its bowl is thought to have been where offerings were placed or incense burned. Behind it is a broad terrace, about 100 feet square, where the outer walls and internal pillars, once supporting a roof, still survive.[9]

To the immediate south of the Temple of the Warriors is what is known as the Thousand Columns, a vast plaza in the shape of an irregular quadrangle over 500 feet on each side. On three sides it is flanked by rows of pillars that once supported an extensive roofing system to create cloisters surrounding a large open-air courtyard. This seems to have been the main meeting place or forum for the citizens of Chichen Itza, and to its immediate south are the remains of what is thought to have been a covered building, some 55 feet square, its vaulted roof once supported by the 24 pedestal columns that still exist. It has been dubbed the Market, as this was once thought to have been its function. However, now that the size of Chichen Itza has been established, this would appear unlikely. As its dimensions seem completely inadequate to accommodate the trading needs of 35,000 inhabitants, it is more likely to have been a meeting hall for the ruling elite or priesthood.[10]

The southern compound is far less extensive than the northern one, containing a second but smaller pyramid called the Osario. Like the Kukulkan Pyramid, it is a step pyramid with staircases on all four sides, although only 30 feet high. There is a temple on top, but unlike the Kukulkan Pyramid, it contains an opening into the main structure that leads to a chamber some 40 feet below, containing human skeletons after which the structure is named. (*Osario* is Spanish for "ossuary," a container or room in which the bones of the dead are housed.) To the south of the Osario is a building dubbed the Observatory, as this is what it is thought to have been. Erected on a 20-foot-high square platform, it is a 30-foot-high round building with a domed roof and cupola, which does bear a striking similarity to modern astronomical observatories, although this one would not have contained a telescope. Instead, its doors and windows are aligned to astronomical events, in particular the path of Venus through the night sky. And to the south of the Osario is a large collection of buildings called Las Monjas (the Nunnery, as this is what the Spanish invaders once thought it was) covered with elaborate texts identifying it as an administrative center. To the west of this is a building, some 160 feet long, 50 feet wide, and 20 feet high, known as the *Akab Dzib,* or "House of Mysterious Writing," because of its intricately carved glyphs identifying it as the palace of the Chichen Itza governor.[11]

These are just some of the many elaborate buildings in the central city complex, which would once have been even more impressive than the gray stone structures still existing today; their statues, bas-reliefs, glyphs, and carvings would have been painted in vivid colors. But Chichen Itza is by no means unique. It was an average-size Mayan city, of which there were around forty, each with between 10,000 and 50,000 inhabitants. At its height, the Mayan empire may have had a population of as many as 10 million. These cities and smaller towns were all connected by elaborate infrastructure with roads as sophisticated as anything built by the Romans. Solid ground would be overlaid by a stratum of large stones, above which was a layer of pebbles, and the surface finished off by a smooth covering of soil. Such a network made it easy to travel through the wild jungle in which the Maya lived.[12] Chichen Itza gives us some idea of what Mayan cities were like. Indeed, the astonishing sophistication of the Mayan civilization served to further persuade the Le Plongeons that there was a link to Atlantis—or, to use what they believed was the Mayan word for lost land—*Mu*.

After the excavations at Chichen Itza, the couple thoroughly examined various Mayan texts searching for references to Mu in works other than the Troano Codex. They found no further allusions to anywhere called Mu, but they were thrilled to discover numerous references to ancient lands lost to the sea. Dating from the seventeenth century, a series of manuscripts collectively referred to as the *Books of Chilam Balam*— "Jaguar Priests"—are illustrated manuscripts written in a Mayan dialect but using the Latin alphabet. These nine surviving texts from various locations throughout the Mayan world were an attempt to preserve Mayan history, religious traditions, as well as what we would now call mythology. Most of them describe the flooding of ancient cities, long ago lost to the sea.[13] Additionally, there was the *Popol Vuh* (Book of the People). This manuscript containing Mayan religious notions, history, and mythology, preserved for centuries in oral tradition, was written around 1550 CE in the hope of conserving Mayan culture at a time when Christian missionaries were busy persuading Native Mesoamericans to forget their past and were destroying their ancient texts. The Le Plongeons were ecstatic to discover that it also contained references to an extensive land that was submerged beneath the waves, just like Atlantis.[14]

For ten years the Le Plongeons visited and photographed dozens of Mayan sites, all the time developing the theory that the original

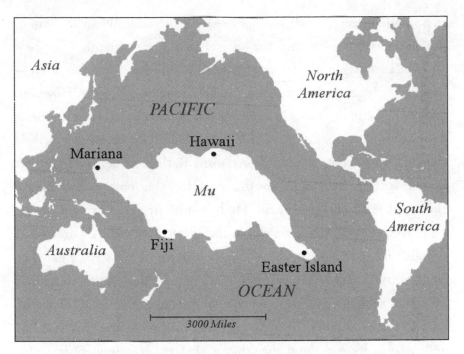

Fig. 3.2. The supposed site of Mu in the Pacific Ocean, showing the locations of modern Mariana, Hawaii, Fiji, and Easter Island.

inhabitants had come from Atlantis. In support of his heartfelt notion that both Mayan and Egyptian civilization began with the lost island, Augustus even expounded the idea that Mayan writing and Egyptian hieroglyphics had a common origin.[15]

However, before they could publish their theories the Le Plongeons were horrified to learn that their work had been hijacked. In 1882, the popularist American author Ignatius Donnelly published his *Atlantis: The Antediluvian World*. Soon a bestseller, it proposed that Atlantis had been the source of both Egyptian and Mayan civilization.[16] Despite Augustus Plongeon writing three volumes between 1886 and 1896 concerning the couple's ideas about the Maya, the Egyptians, and Mu, and Alice writing an epic poem and play about the subject in 1902, Donnelly's work completely eclipsed theirs. His book made the subject of Atlantis enduringly popular, and he differed from the Le Plongeons in proposing that Atlantis was not merely an island, as Plato advocated, but an entire lost continent that once existed in the Atlantic.

The Le Plongeons' work concerning Mu may have been forgotten— were it not for a British engineer named James Churchward. However, unlike the Le Plongeons, Churchward did not accept that Mu had been the Mayan name for Atlantis, and unlike Donnelly, he did not believe that Mu was a continent in the Atlantic. Rather, he believed Mu had been a separate civilization, not in the Atlantic but on the other side of the world in the Pacific Ocean. He had initially been inspired by the Le Plongeons, whom he first met in the 1890s. The three became good friends, and after Augustus Le Plongeon's death in 1908 Alice gave her late husband's papers and research material to Churchward, as he had expressed the desire to write a book on the subject himself. Over the next couple of decades Churchward came to dismiss the idea that Mu and Atlantis were one and the same, and after his retirement in 1926, at the age of 75, he published *The Lost Continent of Mu: Motherland of Man* in which he advocated that Mu had been a separate continent in the Pacific Ocean.

According to Churchward, its inhabitants were an advanced civilization called the Naacal, which flourished from around 50,000 years ago. At its demise around 10,000 BCE, Mu had 64 million inhabitants all following a single religion and one central government. Like Atlantis, Mu had sunk beneath the waves, and not only the Maya but also ancient civilization in India were remnants of its colonies. In Churchward's opinion Mu was a huge continent, extending from Hawaii southeast to Easter Island and southwest to Tonga, incorporating many of the Polynesian Islands, which had once been its mountains. It also included Fiji and what is now Micronesia as far west as the Mariana Islands, making the lost continent about 5,000 miles from east to west and 3,000 miles from north to south, larger than all of South America. Churchward was convinced that direct evidence of its civilization still survived on Easter Island in the form of its *moai*. These huge stone statues of stylized human figures, approximately 900 in all, up to 33 feet high and weighing as much as 80 tons, Churchward believed, had been carved by the ancient Naacal. The sites where it seemed the stone for these monolithic statues had been quarried, around the volcanic crater of Rano Raraku, seemed to have been abruptly abandoned at some time in the past. Discarded stone tools lay scattered all around and unfinished moai still remained awaiting completion, as if the workers had suddenly dropped everything and fled. For Churchward, this was evidence of the great cataclysm that had long ago rapidly and unexpectedly submerged all but Mu's highest land.[17]

So where did James Churchward get all this information, of which Alice and Augustus Le Plongeon appear to have been completely unaware? Evidently, he received it from a Hindu priest while he was in India sometime around 1875. This high-ranking Brahmin supposedly showed him a set of ancient clay tablets in a dead language that could only be read by a handful of people. Somehow, Churchward persuaded the priest to teach him the language and, ultimately, he was not only able to read the priest's texts but also an additional 100 tablets from Mexico. Known as the Niven Tablets, they were discovered by the Scottish archaeologist William Niven in 1921 during a dig in Mexico City.[18]

So, was Mu really a sunken continent supporting an advanced civilization either in the Atlantic or Pacific Ocean? To start with, what about the Le Plongeons' theory, popularized by Ignatius Donnelly, that the Mayan and ancient Egyptian civilizations were related?

Let us start with the pyramids. Indeed, both cultures built what are referred to as pyramids. They were, however, of a very different design. Egyptian pyramids were true, smooth-sided, pointed pyramids, whereas the Mayan "pyramids" were not really pyramids at all. Rather, they consisted of a series of terraces leading to a flat top piazza accommodating a temple building. The early Egyptians did build step pyramids as a precursor to their later, more advanced structures, but they had no buildings on top. Nor is any Egyptian pyramid known to have had stairways up its sides, nor any exterior carving and statuary, as did the Mayan structures. Moreover, the two types of pyramids had completely different functions. Egyptian pyramids were tombs, and the wrongly labeled Mayan pyramids were temples.

Then there are the Mayan glyphs that the Le Plongeons thought resembled Egyptian hieroglyphics. Linguists have since found no such correlation. Egyptian hieroglyphics generally involved individual sounds and concepts represented by a single glyph, written in rows or columns, which can be read from either the left or the right (the direction indicated by the way the animals or human figures face), or from top to bottom. They were read one row or column after another, starting at the same end for a particular text, just as you would do with most modern scripts.[19] But Mayan glyphs were very different. Rather than a single glyph denoting an idea or sound, as with Egyptian hieroglyphics, a block or pair of glyphs represented each concept or sound. And the glyphs are read line by line, alternating from left to right then right to left in an unusual zigzag pattern.[20]

Most damaging to the Le Plongeons' theory is the chronology. Because of modern scientific techniques, such as radiocarbon and pottery dating, we now know with a high degree of accuracy when ancient events occurred—something that was little more than guesswork during the Le Plongeons' time. Archaeologists have determined that ancient Egyptian civilization emerged around 3100 BCE, with the first hieroglyphics dating from around 2700 BCE. The oldest known Egyptian pyramid was built around 2630 BCE.[21] Mayan civilization, on the other hand, did not begin until around 1000 BCE—2,000 years after Egypt—while cities akin to Chichen Itza were not built until about 250 CE. The earliest Mayan writing and stone pyramids date from around the same time—3,000 years after Egypt.[22] Archaeology clearly shows that both cultures and their remarkable achievements developed independently and progressively in situ in their respective regions, with absolutely no need to invoke notions of external influence, either from each other or a lost continent. From what we know today, there is patently no cultural relationship between the Maya and ancient Egyptians. As for Atlantis, we have already discussed how the waters of the Atlantic have been far too deep (an average of over 13,000 feet), and for far too long (millions of years), to have been the location of a sunken continent (see chapter 2). But what about the *Pacific* Mu advocated by James Churchward?

To begin with, mainstream scholars categorically reject Churchward's supposed translation of the Niven Tablets, which officially remained undeciphered until their mysterious disappearance in the 1930s. As for the tablets apparently shown to him by the Indian priest, no one other than Churchward is known to have seen them. We have already examined the unlikelihood of any link between the Mayan and Egyptian civilizations; the same applies to Churchward's idea that there was a connection between the Maya and India. India's earliest true civilization, the Harappan culture in the Indus Valley, only began around 3100 BCE, approximately the same time as Egypt but long before the appearance of Mayan culture. And the earliest form of writing on the Indian subcontinent dates from around 2500 BCE, almost three millennia before the emergence of writing in Mesoamerica.[23] Architectural structures attached to Indian temples were referred to as pyramids during the period of British rule, such as those in Thanjavur, Gangaikonda Cholapuram, and Darasuram, but they bear little or no relationship to those in Egypt or Central America. For instance, they are much steeper and built over temples—more like towers or steeples seen on medieval cathedrals than pyramids. Most damning for Churchward, they only date from around a thousand years ago—11,000 years *after* his continent of Mu is supposed to have sunk beneath the waves.[24] As with ancient Egypt and the Maya, archaeology has revealed indisputable evidence that Indian civilization developed in distinct phases beginning in what is now Pakistan. As with the early Maya, its civilization did not appear fully developed, as would be expected if it came from else-where. Its progress can be clearly identified as occurring progressively on the Indian subcontinent. A lost continent, or influence from Central America, has nothing to do with it.

So, what about the colossal stone statues on Easter Island that Churchward claimed were built by the inhabitants of Mu? Modern dat-ing has revealed that they were built by Polynesian settlers between the thirteenth and sixteenth centuries CE, not a mysterious archaic civiliza-tion that existed tens of millennia ago. The abandonment of the quar-ries at Rano Raraku occurred as recently as 1500 CE—not the 12,000 years in the past proposed by James Churchward.[25] Whatever the reason the builders suddenly dropped tools and deserted the quarries, it was not the cataclysmic flooding of Mu.

Churchward claimed that Mu had been a vast continent, larger than South America, and that its highest mountains still survive as islands and island groups such as Hawaii, Easter Island, Samoa, Tonga, the Cook Islands, Tuvalu, Tokelau, Niue, Wallis, Futuna, and French Polynesia. However, these are volcanic islands that rose from the ocean, not the remains of a continent that existed in water with a mean depth of two and a half miles. Like the Atlantic, the open Pacific is far too deep to have supported a continent in the entire history of *Homo sapiens*. Interestingly, though, there was a small landmass about half the size of Australia in the southwest Pacific, the surviving remnants of which are New Zealand and New Caledonia. However, even *it* sub-merged by around 23 million years ago—long before Churchward's Mu civilization was purportedly founded—at a time when the living human predecessors were the Dryopithecines, the common ape ancestors we share with chimpanzees.

Nevertheless, although there may not have been lost civilizations in the Atlantic or Pacific, nor any link between the Mayan civilization and those in Egypt or India, the Mayan texts consulted by the Le Plongeons, Donnelly, and Churchward do indeed refer to lands being lost to the sea at some time in the remote past. Interestingly, these researchers seem to have completely overlooked that these texts provide a specific location for these events (maybe deliberately, because they pretty much refute any link to the supposed lands of Atlantis or Mu). According to the *Books of Chilam Balam,* a great flood overcame the first settlements of an early people on the coast of Soconusco, a narrow strip of land between the Sierra Madre de Chiapas Mountains and the Pacific Ocean in the southwest corner of Mexico.[26] A similar account is found in the *Popol Vuh,* in which an early civilization in Soconusco was destroyed in a flood summoned by two demigods called the Hero Twins, forcing that culture to develop again from scratch, ultimately giving rise to the Maya.[27] We have already seen that worldwide sea levels rose by some 100 feet between 7000 and 4000 BCE, and during that period, by around 5000 BCE, people known as the Mokaya had established permanent early farming communities along the Soconusco Strip. Archaeological excavations in 1948, 1955, 1975, and 1991 all found the foundations of multiple concentrations of round and rectangular dwellings, accompanied by sophisticated pottery, shell and gemstone ornamentations, and obsidian tools.[28] The Mokaya left behind no huge stone structure like the Maya, but they did create some of the world's so-called first cities with complex wooden or mudbrick buildings sharing features with those at Erbil Citadel and Jericho in the Middle East, Plovdiv and Belovode in Europe, Huaca Prieta and Monte Verde in South America, and Jiahu and Mehrgarh in Asia (recall chapter 2). The coastal Mokaya towns were fishing settlements close to the shoreline, and those that existed in the fifth millennium BCE would certainly have been submerged as sea levels rose by some 30 feet between 5000 and 4000 BCE. In fact, in 1995 archaeologists Barbara Voorhies and Douglas Kennett of the University of California concluded that many early Mokaya settlements had been lost to the sea along the Soconusco coast. Unfortunately, because they were not constructed of durable stone, it is likely that all evidence of them will have been obliterated by 6,000 years beneath the waves.[29]

Around 1600 BCE the descendants of the Mokaya people founded the first true civilization in Central America. Known as the Olmec—famous for their sculptures of colossal stone heads (without upper torsos, like those later erected on Easter Island)—they built numerous cities, roads, aqueducts, irrigation channels, drainage systems, and even had domestic plumbing.[30] One of the largest Olmec cities was San Lorenzo, with around 13,000 inhabitants. Here, like other Olmec cities, the elite lived in lavish structures erected on raised terraces. For example, the so-called Red Palace had 16-inch-thick mudbrick, plastered walls, ceilings supported by 13-foot-high basalt columns, and floors made from gravel overlaid with leveled, hard-packed clay. The city was supplied with fresh water by hundreds of covered, carved basalt troughs, each weighing many tons, quarried from as far away as 50 miles. No form of writing now survives to document their beliefs, but they seem to have been the forebears of the Maya. It is generally agreed that the Olmec directly gave rise to the Maya, as there are many Olmec precursors to features found in Mayan civilization. Although no Olmec temples are known to survive intact, the culture did build flat-topped, pyramid-shaped earthen mounds, atop of which archaeologists have discovered the foundations of large wooden buildings. It is believed that these were the forerunners of the Mayan stone, stepped pyramids, and their apex temples. And the discovery of ball courts demonstrates that the Olmec played, and probably invented, the Ōllamaliztli ball game that was so popular with the later Maya.

Among Olmec ruins carvings and statues of feathered serpents have been found, remarkably like the Mayan depictions of their chief god Kukulkan.[31] Just outside San Lorenzo is El Azuzul, thought to have been a religious site. There survives a huge mound, likely an early Olmec pyramid temple, which has at its base two adjacent, identical statues of kneeling men. These statues, known as the Twins, still survive, and are thought to be the forerunners of the Mayan Hero Twins from the *Popul Vuh*. Moreover, the Olmec, who eventually ruled over most of southern Mexico and Guatemala, declined at precisely the time the Maya rose to prominence in that very area.[32]

As we saw in chapter 1, ancient peoples without writing are known to have handed down oral traditions for millennia, as indeed the Mokaya may have with accounts of the flooding of early settlements on the Soconusco coastline between 5000 and 4000 BCE. And their descendants, the Olmec, may well have continued such narratives by word of mouth, narratives that would ultimately be committed to writing by their successors, the Maya. It seems, then, that the Mayan tales of ancient, flooded lands—although not concerning lost islands or continents—may well refer to sunken coastal regions of the Soconusco Strip, submerged beneath the Pacific by around 6,000 years ago. But was this region called Mu? The only supposed reference to this as the name of a flooded land was found in the Troano Codex by Charles Étienne Brasseur de Bourbourg in 1864, and subsequently adopted by the Le Plongeons, James Churchward, and others. Although the Mayan language was at least partly understood in the nineteenth century, due to it surviving in various Mexican dialects, Mayan glyphs were not properly deciphered until the 1980s. Modern translations of the Troano Codex—now known as the Madrid Codex after the city where it is kept—have revealed that it was not a work concerning ancient history, as earlier scholars believed, but an astrological treatise.[33] Consequently, any reference to floods concerned such cataclysms predicted to occur in the *future*. As for the word *Mu*, it appears nowhere in the manuscript. The glyphs de Bourbourg deciphered as *Mu,* which he apparently learned from a Mayan dialect speaker, are now known to be *muk*—pronounced "myook," not "myoo"—which means "to bury." It seems that the relevant passage concerned an unnamed location predicted to *one day* be buried by a flood, not a land called Mu that had *long ago* sunk beneath the sea.[34]

So, the purported continents of Atlantis and Mu most likely originated with ancient oral accounts respectively referring to a small island in the eastern Atlantic near the Strait of Gibraltar and a strip of land along the Pacific coastline of Mexico and Guatemala, each supporting the kind of sizable farming settlements referred to by scholars as the world's "first cities." The former was submerged by a massive tidal wave, and the latter gradually succumbed to rising sea levels, both directly due to global warming.

There is also, however, a third hypothetical sunken continent, this one supposedly in the Indian Ocean. Known as Lemuria, this huge continent is said to have been a landmass stretching from southern India to the large island of Madagascar off the southeast coast of Africa—making it over 3,000 miles wide. First proposed in 1864 by the English zoologist Philip Sclater, the original theory seemed quite acceptable for the time, even among academics. In an article titled "The Mammals of Madagascar" in the respected British scientific periodical *Quarterly Journal of Science,* Sclater drew attention to the presence of distinctive Madagascan fauna and flora being found in fossils from southern India. The only explanation, he concluded, was that the two locations were once linked by a land bridge. He expediently called this 3,000-mile-wide landmass Lemuria, after the lemurs, a species of ring-tailed primates unique to Madagascar, as fossils of a common ancestor were found on both the island and in India. Two decades after Sclater's proposal, the renowned Russian occultist and mystic Helena Blavatsky proposed that Lemuria had

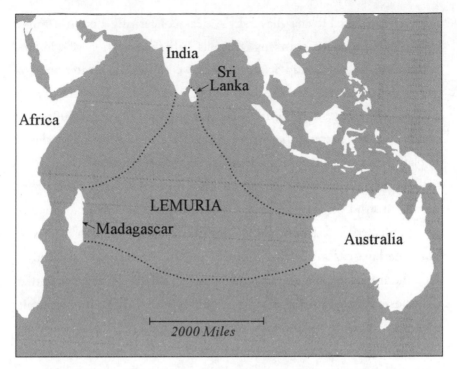

Fig. 3.3. The supposed location of Lemuria in the Indian Ocean.

not merely been a land bridge but an entire continent that extended between southern India, western Australia, and Madagascar, and had been the homeland of an advanced civilization destroyed when volcanic activity caused the land to sink beneath the waves around four million years ago. Even though many of Blavatsky's admirers are still convinced by the history of Lemuria revealed in her book *The Secret Doctrine,* published in 1888, which she claimed to have learned from ancient Tibetan manuscripts, most scholars remain skeptical, to say the least.[35] As with James Churchward's supposed Mu tablets from India, Blavatsky's Tibetan texts were never produced for examination. Moreover, she made claims that many would now consider to be absurd. For example, she proposed that Lemurian civilization began during the age of the dinosaurs and that the Lemurians reproduced by laying eggs.

Even though Helena Blavatsky's ideas concerning Lemuria might seem silly to modern thinking, there is still the question of the land bridge theorized by Philip Sclater. Today we know that Sclater was correct in deducing that fossils from Madagascar and India were related, but geologists have determined that this was not due to a 3000-mile land bridge, but because the two locations were once joined. The theory of plate tectonics—the movement of discrete sections of the Earth's crust known as plates, made from hard rock called the lithosphere, moving around on a softer underlayer known as the asthenosphere— has established that around 70 million years ago the Indian plate split from Madagascar and drifted slowly northeast, ultimately colliding with the Eurasian plate about 35 million years later. There, the Indian plate pushed up against the coast of what is now Tibet, forcing up its land like a gigantic bulldozer to create the Himalayas.[36]

Although we now know that there was no ancient continent of Lemuria, during the late nineteenth century certain scholars among the Tamil people of Sri Lanka and southern India adapted the popular Lemuria hypothesis to account for their mythology concerning Kumari Kandam, a sunken realm said to have been their ancient homeland.[37] However, earlier Tamil tradition did not regard the place as a continent but a submerged land that once joined the Tamil regions of Sri Lanka and southern India. The oldest surviving reference to the land of Kumari Kandam by that name appeared around the year 1400 CE in the *Kanda Puranam*, a Tamil translation of a fifth-century Sanskrit text, the *Skanda Purana*.[38] In it, we learn that *kandam* meant "land" and *Kumari* was the name of its legendary first queen: "the Land of Queen Kumari." Various medieval Tamil writers, such as Ilampuranar and Perasiriyar, mention other now-missing manuscripts that refer to land lost to the sea off the coast of southern India, while the thirteenth-century commentator on ancient Indian texts, Adiyarku Nallar, implies that this land joined southeastern

India with the island of Sri Lanka.[39] Much of the seabed between
northwest Sri Lanka and India, now the Palk Strait—which measures
120 miles north to south by 150 miles east to west (18,000 square
miles in all)—has a mean depth of just about 40 feet, the known
rise in sea level after the Ice Age, indicating that it was above water
until around 5000 BCE (see chapter 1). So, there was indeed a lost
land where Kumari Kandam was originally thought to have been, but
whether it supported early settlements is presently unknown.

In conclusion, we have seen how throughout the world there exist
ancient accounts of coastal lands and islands lost to rising sea levels due
to global warming after the Ice Age. In examining lost civilizations, we
can theorize and appreciate how advanced and complex a society on
North Doggerland could have been. We now turn to another category
of early narratives that may also be explained by postglacial climate
change: those concerning the so-called Deluge or Great Flood.

4
The Great Flood
. . . .
Stories from Ancient Civilizations

To further provide some idea as to the cataclysms of the postglacial world in which the civilization on Doggerland perilously lived, we turn to ancient narratives referring to a *worldwide* flood that can be found in the mythology of many of the earliest civilizations. Before examining these accounts, we should define what is meant by the term *civilization* in this context. Basically, the term refers to a complex society characterized by urban centers or cities, an intricate social hierarchy, peacekeeping forces or armies, an elaborate communication structure typified by roads, and writing or some symbolic transmission of information. In most respects, early civilizations were far more elaborate and technologically more advanced than the urbian, "first city" settlements that preceded them (such as those discussed in chapter 2). The earliest true civilizations we know of were Sumer, centered on southern Iraq; ancient Egypt in North Africa; and the Indus Valley culture in Pakistan and northwest India. As they had much in common, for the purposes of this investigation we need only consider one in any detail to appreciate just how much they differed from what existed before. So, let's examine what is generally agreed to have been the first: Sumer, the civilization usually credited with inventing the wheel, writing, and mathematics.

Beginning around 3300 BCE, the Sumer civilization arose in the southernmost part of Mesopotamia, a historical region within the Tigris-Euphrates river system in what is now Iraq. The civilization probably arose due to the invention of the alloy bronze, the first hard-wearing metal, which was used to make heavy-duty weapons and tools. Sumer consisted of several cities about 250 acres in size, each with populations of approximately 10,000. The capital, Uruk, was much bigger, almost 1,000 acres in size, with more than 50,000 inhabitants. These cities were linked not only by waterways but also by an extensive network of roads, while the surrounding fields were irrigated by an ingenious system of artificial channels. Each city had temples for the priesthood, palaces for local rulers, and public buildings for centralized administration. Metal molding saw the development of all manner of new implements: fine needles for sewing, devices for weaving, chisels for carving, and the stylus for forming designs in clay. The development of the metal stylus, a small tool for intricate marking and shaping, led to the invention of writing by imprinting soft clay with symbols denoting objects, life forms, concepts, and verbal sounds. The birth of writing meant that communications were vastly improved. Orders, proclamations, and ideas could be disseminated on clay tablets, easily made and transported, and monuments could be inscribed with records, ideologies, mythology, and religious notions, together with the exploits of leaders and the ruling elite. Sumer is said to be the first place on Earth to emerge from prehistory into the era of history, the period from which written records survive.[1]

Besides having large and comfortable homes, and forces to keep law and order in the streets outside, citizens of Sumer enjoyed the benefits of many domestic items previously undreamed of. Early pots had been made by coiling and rolling clay into long threads and pinching them together to form vessels, but the invention of the potter's wheel, turned by hand or foot, made pottery-making faster and more efficient, enabling the industrial production of ceramic ware. City dwellers not only had decent furniture, thanks to the advances in carpentry by using metal tools, but they also had the kind of everyday crockery—pots, plates, cups, and storage vessels—we now take for granted. And they had metal cutlery too, which meant they no longer had to eat with their hands.

Status in society could be expressed through various ornamentations unheard of elsewhere in the world. Adornments made from shells, bones, and stones were commonly worn throughout the Neolithic period, but metalworking took personal decorations to another level. Along with the manufacture of bronze, gold and silver were also smelted to produce sophisticated ornaments such as bracelets, necklaces, and rings, together with household items like platters, drinking vessels, and statuettes. Also, the cutting, shaping, and polishing of precious stones developed on a commercial scale, meaning that many more people could wear jewelry.[2]

The two other civilizations that began around the same time—in Egypt by 3150 BCE, and in the Indus Valley by 3000 BCE—also arose using bronze. Although architectural style and religious beliefs differed, both civilizations had very similar societal structures and levels of technology to the Sumerians. And, of primary interest here, despite being separated by thousands of miles all three of these civilizations left written accounts of an ancient, worldwide flood.

The oldest account, from Sumer, is found in *The Epic of Ziusudra,* in which we are told that well before the birth of Sumerian civilization the gods decided to punish humanity by flooding the world. The water god Enki warns Ziusudra, king of Shuruppak in southern Iraq, of the coming deluge, instructing him to build a huge boat. After a terrible storm that floods the world, Ziusudra's boat comes to rest on a mountain and he and his family are saved. He then erects an altar in Enki's honor.[3] Thereafter, according to the *Sumerian King List* compiled sometime during the third millennium BCE, Ziusudra and his successors ruled from the new city of Kish, some 50 miles northwest of Shuruppak.[4] While it contains clearly mythological elements, the tale may well be based on actual events that occurred 2,500 years before the emergence of Sumerian civilization. Although archaeology has revealed that Shuruppak was not occupied until around 3000 BCE, Kish dates from very much earlier. The site of the city, at modern Tell al-Uhaymir in Iraq, has been thoroughly excavated to determine it was occupied as an urbian settlement of some 570 acres between 7,500 and 6,500 years ago.[5] Accordingly, if the account has any historicity, it would seem to have been set at the time Kish was first occupied, sometime around 5500 BCE, during the period when sea levels were rising between 7000 and 4000 BCE.

In 2010, archaeologist Jeffrey Rose from the University of Birmingham in the UK proposed that a low-lying fertile plane, adjoining

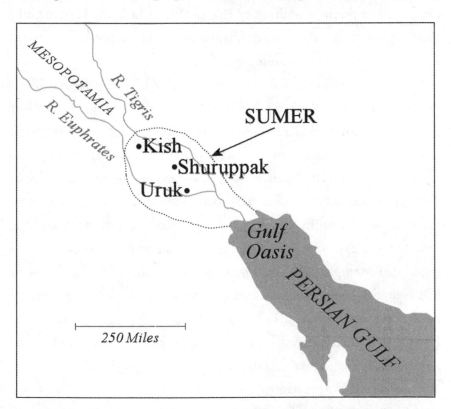

Fig. 4.1. The Sumer civilization and the location of the Gulf Oasis.

the southern tip of Mesopotamia and stretching some 120 miles out to sea, probably supported an early culture until it was completely submerged beneath the waters of the Persian Gulf by 5500 BCE. Recently, archaeologists have uncovered evidence of a surge of human settlements being established in the area that later became Sumer dating from precisely that time, when the fertile plain was finally engulfed. As there is no previous evidence of these people elsewhere in the region, it is likely that they migrated from this sunken land, which archaeologists refer to as the Gulf Oasis. One such settlement was the early city of Kish, where the Sumerians believed a new line of kings was established after the Great Flood. Although experts now know that the entire world was not flooded at this time, to the people who long ago dwelled in the Gulf Oasis it must have seemed that way. On examining the evidence for the existence of a precursor culture on this sunken land in the Persian Gulf, Rose suggested that the Sumerian flood myth may well have originated with this historical inundation event.[6]

Soon after the Sumerian civilization emerged, the Egyptian civilization appeared around 1000 miles to the west along the northern River Nile. The region had already grown prosperous due to the life-giving river and the spreading rivulet system of the Nile Delta, but once the inhabitants mastered the manufacture of bronze, significant cultural changes followed. Powerful armies wielding bronze weapons facilitated the creation of a unified nation with centralized government, and the kingdom of Egypt was born. Egyptian civilization was founded around the city of Memphis, about 20 miles south of modern Cairo. The city had around 30,000 inhabitants, and towns under its control were linked by the Nile and its vast array of rivulets. By about 3150 BCE ancient Egypt had gained nearly all the benefits of civilization enjoyed by the Sumerians, including writing in the form of hieroglyphics.[7]

Like Sumer, Egypt had its Deluge myth. Accounts of a global flood are found in the *Book of the Dead,* an ancient Egyptian text with copies written on papyrus (an early form of paper) dating from around 1550 BCE.[8] However, sections of the script are found inscribed in much earlier tombs, the oldest being the so-called Pyramid Texts carved into the chambers and sarcophagi of the pyramids of Giza between 2600 and 2500 BCE.[9] In this ancient narrative we learn that in some remote period of the past the sun god Ra grew weary of the transgressions of humanity, and to bring them in line sent his daughter Sekhmet to wreak havoc upon the Earth. Ra only intended for her to inflict limited devastation, but once the goddess got going, she refused to stop. Sekhmet eventually flooded much of the world before Ra interceded. By the time the *Book of the Dead* was standardized in the second millennium BCE, the story

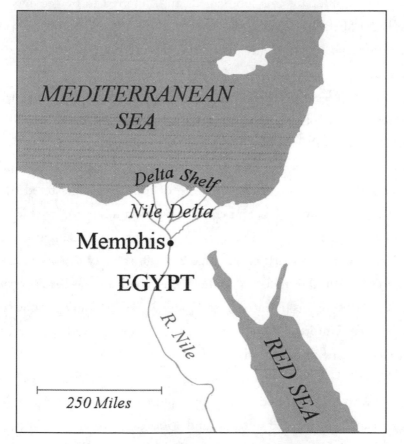

Fig. 4.2. Ancient Egypt and the Delta Shelf.

concerned the world being flooded with blood or beer, but earlier tomb texts refer simply to a dreadful inundation that implies water.

As in southern Mesopotamia, Egypt suffered a catastrophic loss of land between 8,500 and 7,500 years ago due to rising sea levels. In the 1990s, core samples taken from the seabed off the Nile Delta by a team led by Jean-Daniel Stanley, curator of sedimentology at the Smithsonian National Museum of Natural History, revealed that the coast of pre-dynastic Egypt once stretched about 30 miles farther out into the Mediterranean than it does today. Layers of sediment extracted from the sea floor have preserved deposits of vegetation that only grow on land dating up until approximately 5500 BCE.[10] It's possible, then, that oral accounts of this submerged land, referred to by geologists as the Delta Shelf, were passed down from those forced to migrate south into mainland Egypt, eventually morphing into the myth of Sekhmet's Great Flood.

The third early civilization to arise around the same time as Sumer and Egypt was the Indus Valley culture of northwest India and Pakistan. Like the Nile Delta and Mesopotamia, the Indus Valley was a region made fertile by a major river system, in its case the Indus River and its tributaries. The smelting of bronze was mastered by its people around 3000 BCE, and civilization soon followed. Its chief city was located at Harappa, in modern Sindh province. Occupying about 400 acres with a population of some 25,000, the city lent its name to the archaeological term for the Indus Valley civilization—the *Harappan* culture. Writing was invented in the Indus Valley around the same time as smelting. Unfortunately, however, Indus script, as Harappan writing is called, has never been translated.[11]

Nonetheless, like Egypt and Sumer, India's oldest readable texts also refer to a worldwide flood occurring sometime in the remote past. The Harappan culture lasted until around 1500 BCE, when Hindu people from the northeast, from what is now Punjab, occupied the area. It was here, at this very time, that India's oldest translatable scripts, the Vedas, were composed in Sanskrit, the liturgical language of Hinduism. They include recurring accounts of a great, worldwide flood, possibly taken from earlier Harappan texts before the knowledge to translate them was lost.[12] The earliest renderings of such accounts are incomplete, with the oldest full renditions appearing in commentaries on the Vedas by Hindu sages, such as Yajnavalkya of Kosala who lived around the eighth century BCE. In the *Shatapatha Brahmana* (*Instruction of a Hundred Paths*) Yajnavalkya describes how the god Vishnu warns certain righteous men and their families of a coming flood that will cover the Earth. They build boats and so are saved to repopulate the world.[13]

If such narratives were borrowed from the Harappans, then they could in turn have originated with oral accounts passed down from the pre-Harappan population of the Indus Valley, the so-called Mehrgarh culture, named after an archaeological site near the Pakistani city of Quetta. The Mehrgarh people existed in the region from around 7000 BCE but abruptly transformed into an early urbian culture around 5500 BCE— the so-called Mehrgarh II period—with the making of ceramics and durable mud bricks, unknown in the region before this age. Their technological innovations were truly spectacular for the time. They even mastered the smelting of copper. Although not so hard as bronze (an alloy of copper and tin), copper enabled the Mehrgarh people to produce some of the world's first metal utensils, such as saws, needles, pincers, scissors, and drill bits.[14] Astonishingly, archaeologists have discovered the world's earliest evidence of dentistry in this region dating from the Mehrgarh II period, human remains revealing teeth that had been drilled and filled.[15]

As there is no archaeological evidence that these sudden innovations came from the north, it is generally thought that they originated with a prosperous fishing society that once existed in the coastal region of the Indus Delta.[16] Like the Mesopotamian Gulf Oasis and the Egyptian Delta Shelf, a large landmass known as the Indus Shelf, off the present

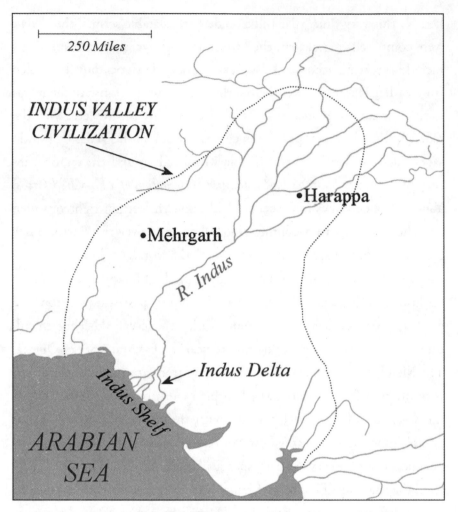

Fig. 4.3. The Indus Valley civilization and the Indus Shelf.

mouth of the Indus, stretching about 30 miles out into the Arabian Sea, was gradually flooded by rising sea levels up until it was finally submerged around 5500 BCE—the very time that the innovative Mehrgarh II period began in the Indus Valley.[17] The Mehrgarh culture survived until around 3500 BCE, when it transformed into the Harappa civilization—and so accounts of this flooding, which forced the inhabitants of the Indus Shelf to migrate north and invigorate the Mehrgarh culture, could well have been behind the Great Flood narratives in Hindu mythology.[18]

Along with ancient Deluge stories originally inspired by rising sea levels, there are also such accounts initiated by the long-term rise in river levels due to increased rainfall. (A warmer climate increased the evaporation of water, resulting in higher rainfall in many areas. Also, many regions had less snowfall, meaning that more atmospheric water precipitated as rain, rather than remaining as permanent snow cover in the mountains.)

An excellent example is the ancient Chinese story of *The Great Flood of Gun-Yu*. The story is set in and around a supposedly great city in the Yi-Luo basin in modern Henan Province. In some remote era of the past, we are told, river waters gradually rose, forcing increasing numbers of people to leave their homes to live on higher ground. Eventually the rising waters threaten the city itself, until two engineers—Gun and his son Yu—find a solution. For many years the city is saved after the pair organize the construction of a series of ditches, embankments, and channels to hold back and redirect flood waters, but ultimately the defenses fail, and the city is swamped.[19] Like the deluge myths of Sumer, Egypt, and the Indus Valley, the version of the *Gun-Yu* story from the period of Imperial China, following the late third century BCE, refers to the Great Flood ultimately engulfing the entire world. The oldest surviving rendition, however, found in the *Yáo diǎn* (*Canon of Yao*) composed around 1000 BCE, only concerns the flooding of the Yi-Luo basin.[20] And it was here that the events described in *The Great Flood of Gun-Yu* really do seem to have occurred around 5500 BCE. Before examining this, we need to appreciate that Chinese proto-civilization seems to have started well before it did in Sumer, Egypt, and the Indus Valley.

China is different from many other early civilizations in that its buildings have not survived, even as visible foundations. This is because they were generally built from wood and other perishable materials like bamboo because of the abundance of forests in the subtropical birthplace of Chinese culture. The kinds of trees that flourish here grow extraordinary fast, quickly replenishing resources. For example, the paulownia tree, a species of hardwood that can grow to over 100 feet, produces strong, lightweight timber with a high strength-to-weight ratio, ideal for use as a building material. It can grow up to 20 feet in a single year and be harvested for timber within as little as five years. Paulownias don't even need to be replanted from seed. Once cut down, they regrow from their existing root systems. Then there's bamboo, one of the fastest-growing plants on Earth, which can reach maturity within as little as three months. One species can grow an astonishing 3 feet in a single day. It wasn't until between 475 and 221 BCE, during a period of warring between separate Chinese states, that brickmaking began, primarily for building defensive structures. When China was united into a single empire by Qin Shi Huang (the emperor eventually buried with the famous Terracotta Army) in 221 BCE, a truly massive stone and brick structure, the Great Wall of China, was built to defend the empire from hostile peoples to the north.[21]

However, because the foundations of stone and brick buildings were not found dating from before the fifth century BCE, western archaeologists long considered Chinese civilization to date back to no earlier than two and a half thousand years ago. But modern archaeology has shown this to be woefully wrong. Scientific techniques to identify the foundations of wooden structures in the soil, determining a building's size, shape, weight, and even original height, have revealed complex and highly organized Chinese cities dating from much earlier. It now seems that the Chinese were building cities evincing a highly sophisticated society dating from as many as 3,500 years before the civilizations of Sumer, Egypt, and the Indus Valley. Known as the Peiligang culture, which flourished between 7000 and 5000 BCE, its cities were smaller than these other early civilizations, with around 1,000 inhabitants in each. But there were more cities, and they were closer together. Over a hundred have so far been identified in the Yi-Luo basin around the Yellow River in modern Henan Province. They were more advanced than other contemporary cities, such as the urban settlements we examined in chapter 2, with superior ceramics and more elaborate implements. They even had an early form of writing: pictograms carved into bone, shells, pottery, and clay tablets appear to have been the origins of later Chinese characters.[22] And it may well be because the Chinese developed writing much earlier than other cultures that its flood stories survived in detail relatively unfettered by later mythology.

As noted, events described in *The Great Flood of Gun-Yu* really do seem to have occurred around 7,700 years ago. To begin with, the story tells how for many years people were progressively forced to leave their homes to live on higher ground. And this is exactly what archaeology has revealed happened to the Peiligang culture for some time prior to 5700 BCE. Archaeology has revealed a considerable increase in population of higher-elevation settlements in the Yi-Luo basin during the early sixth century BCE. Rivers changed course due to rising water levels fed by long-term higher rainfall, imperiling lower-lying areas. The *Gun-Yu* goes on to relate how ditches, embankments, and channels were constructed to hold back flooding around the principal city in the region until the defenses were eventually breached. Remarkably, archaeology at the site of Jiahu—one the largest known settlements of the Peiligang culture—has revealed that it was surrounded by a network of precisely such earthworks, dug around 7,700 years ago to prevent flooding from the Sha River, which was encroaching upon the city from the north. But by 5500 BCE the defenses ultimately failed, and the city was submerged—but only for a while. Within a few years silting caused the Sha to change course, thus preserving the historical site. Thereafter, the river ran south of Jiahu, as it does today, enabling modern archaeological work.[23]

Perhaps the most notorious of the ancient Deluge accounts comes from the Bible, in the story of Noah's Ark found in the Book of

Genesis.[24] Here we are told that, because of their misdeeds, God resolves to destroy humanity with a worldwide flood. He instructs the world's only just man, Noah, to build a great boat, the Ark, in which he, his family, and a breeding pair of all the world's animals are to ride out the storm. When the flood eventually abates, the Ark comes to rest upon "the mountains of Ararat,"[25] and those aboard are saved to repopulate the Earth.

The story is generally assumed to have been taken from Babylonian mythology at the time when many Jewish people were held captive in Babylon, between 597 and 539 BCE. Babylon was in Mesopotamia and its flood myth, found in the Babylonian *Epic of Gilgamesh,* is a retelling of the earlier Sumerian *Epic of Ziusudra* (previously discussed).[26] In the Mesopotamian story, the god Enki, and in the biblical account, the Hebrew God, decide to destroy mankind because of its wickedness. In both accounts a sole, righteous man is chosen to build a huge boat and he, his family, and various animals are saved. Both vessels come to rest on a high mountain, and both Ziusudra and Noah immediately give thanks by building an altar where they make burnt offerings. But there is an important difference: in the *Ziusudra* and *Gilgamesh* narratives the mountain where the boat comes to rest is in the land of Dilmun, modern day Bahrain to the south of Mesopotamia, whereas the Genesis account has Noah's Ark coming to rest on the mountains of Ararat in what is now Armenia and northeast Turkey, at the eastern end of the Black Sea. It has accordingly been argued that the story of Noah, although drawing upon later Mesopotamian mythology, was originally inspired by a flood that devastated early settlements surrounding the Black Sea.

There is a mountain in the extreme east of Turkey now called Mount Ararat, but it has only been so named since the Middle Ages, when Christians of the Byzantine Empire deduced it to be the place where Noah's Ark came to rest. *Ararat,* however, was the

Hebrew name for the ancient kingdom of Urartu, which existed in what was later Greater Armenia (today, an area including modern Armenia and northeast Turkey) between the ninth and sixth centuries BCE. Accordingly, the words from the Genesis account, "mountains of Ararat," seem to refer to what are now called the Armenian Highlands. Around the year 450 CE, the Armenian historian Movses Khorenatsi composed the earliest known history of Armenia written in the Armenian language. In his *Patmut'yun Hayots* (*History of Armenia*), he collated the various oral and legendary traditions of his country's origins into this single work, in which he says that his countryfolk long believed that Noah and his family had resided in the Armenian Highlands.[27] These highlands overlook the eastern end of the Black Sea, and in the late twentieth century a theory was proposed that here, around 5500 BCE, early settlements were indeed subjected to a devastating flood of truly biblical proportions.

In 1997 a team led by geophysicist William Ryan and geologist Walter Pitman of Columbia University, together with oceanographer Petko Dimitrov of the Bulgarian Academy of Sciences, published their Black Sea deluge hypothesis. They argued that following the Ice Age, the Black Sea was a huge freshwater lake separated from the Mediterranean by a rocky barrier or natural dam at the Bosporus. By the sixth century BCE the waters of the Mediterranean had risen to 260 feet higher than the lake beyond the barrier, and around 5500 BCE the barrier was finally breached. According to the team, the barrier collapsed in a catastrophic landslide, and an enormous waterfall, two hundred times the flow of Niagara Falls, surged into the lake from the Mediterranean via the Sea of Marmara, pulverizing the shoreline and inundating the countryside for miles inland over a truly vast area. Loss of life for the fishing settlements and early farming communities around the huge lake must have been colossal. The hellish cascade lasted for around ten months, until water levels equalized,

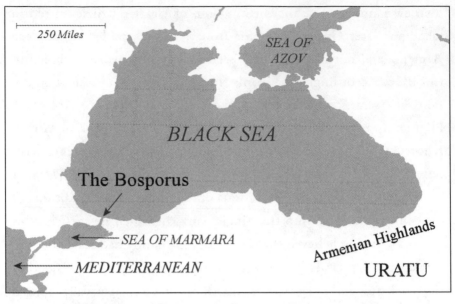

Fig. 4.4. The Black Sea and the locations likely associated with the biblical Great Flood.

and the lake became the Black Sea, connected to the Mediterranean by the Bosporus Strait. As the Black Sea was now vastly larger than the original lake and 260 feet higher, huge swathes of land would have been submerged at a time when Neolithic lakeside settlements would have been abundant. The memory of such an enormous cataclysm, the researchers suggested, may have lived on to become the story of Noah's flood.[28]

We have examined just a few of the Great Flood myths from early civilizations, but there are many more global deluge tales preserved in mythology from around the world, in ancient Scandinavian, Polynesian, Native American, African, Asian, and European traditions.[29] Like the myths of Sumer, Egypt, the Indus Valley, and Armenia, many such narratives appear to have developed from oral accounts of *local* flooding. So why the insistence that such floods covered the entire world, engulfing even the highest mountains? There is certainly no geological evidence that such an event, or anything remotely like it, has ever happened in the entire history of planet Earth. There's nowhere near enough water, for a start. Even if all the ice covering Antarctica, Greenland, and the world's mountain glaciers melted, sea levels would only rise by about 230 feet above what they are now. If, additionally, all the water in the atmosphere somehow fell to earth, barely 0.001 percent more water would be added to the new seas—hardly a drop in the ocean. Although apocalyptically tragic for modern civilization, only around 10 percent of the Earth's land would be underwater. In fact, throughout the age of the dinosaurs this is close to what sea levels were.[30] (Scientists contend that the world did freeze over a couple of times more than half a billion years ago, but that was mainly surface ice created by impacted snow. Even though the oceans were covered in surface ice, most of the world's land was still above sea level.) Despite what various religious factions believe, from the scientific perspective there never was a Great Flood that covered the world.

In the late fifteenth century, none other than Leonardo da Vinci may have first solved the mystery around the widespread belief in an ancient global flood. In his notebooks he records that he found petrified shells in the rocks of mountains in the Lombardy region of Italy, which the Church cited as evidence for Noah's flood. Leonardo, however, had a different idea. Reasoning that such shells would have to have been scattered by such a deluge, not gathered into groups as they were on the Lombardy mountains, he theorized that the remains of these marine creatures had been laid down in sediment at the bottom of seas and lakes, and that the land had subsequently risen.[31] He had no explanation as to how such a geological event might occur, but the theory of plate tectonics developed during the 1950s and '60s proved him right. Over millions of years, the seismic movement of the Earth's crust does thrust up vast expanses of rock strata that were once ancient seafloors to form mountain ranges. We now know this is how the shells Leonardo observed—now called fossils—found their way to the top of mountains.

And such fossils can be found on high ground all around the world. It is quite likely that ancient peoples also observed fossils on high ground, and arrived at the same conclusion as the medieval Church: there had once been a flood that covered even the highest land. American historian Adrienne Mayor of Stanford University, who theorizes that global flood stories were inspired by the fossils of ancient sea creatures observed at high elevation, has referenced Greek, Roman, and Egyptian texts documenting the discovery and interpretation of such finds. The Greeks, for example, deduced from such fossils that the Earth had been covered completely by water on several occasions.[32]

We have seen how rising temperatures during the urbian and proto-civilization eras, between 7000 and 4000 BCE, caused a rise in sea and river levels resulting in the widespread submergence and relocation of early human settlements—a geological and archaeological reality reflected in the extensive flood mythology from ancient civilizations around the world. (A more comprehensive timeline detailing when North Doggerland may have been submerged is given in chapter 6.) We turn now to another, perhaps more terrifying and seemingly unlikely consequence of Neolithic global warming—pandemics and disease.

5
Melting Ice, Climate Change, and Pandemics

....

Their Impacts on Urbian Populations around the World

The world in which the Doggerland civilization lived was suffering from other terrifying effects of climate change. Investigating these effects on civilizations around the world allows us to theorize how the people of Doggerland may have fared in the face of climate change. Looking at the global picture, it's likely the Doggerland civilization experienced more than just a change in climate.

For convenience, I have been using the term *Ice Age* for the period of low global temperatures from which humanity emerged around 12,000 years ago. Technically, however, the Ice Age has not ended. The Arctic (northern) ice sheet, which covers most of Greenland, averages just under one and a half miles thick, and is three times the size of Texas. But that is nothing compared to the Antarctic (southern) ice sheet. As much as 3 miles deep, it covers an entire continent the size of the United States and Mexico combined. At present, permanent ice covers around 10 percent of the Earth's surface, and in geological terms that constitutes an ice age. During the Eocene epoch, which lasted from 56 to 34 million years ago, the world experienced mean annual temperatures of 29.4 degrees Celsius (85 degrees Fahrenheit), compared with today's 14.4 degrees Celsius (58 degrees Fahrenheit). Even Antarctica had an average yearly temperature of 13.8 degrees Celsius (57 degrees Fahrenheit), as warm as the modern state of Washington. After the Eocene epoch, world temperatures began to slowly drop until the Quaternary period, which started around two and a half million years ago. (The term *glaciation* refers not only to glaciers but also to ice sheets.) From this time, the world has seen glaciation cycles of advancing and retreating ice known respectively as *glacials* and *interglacials*. Glacials, when ice sheets have covered much of North America, Russia, and northern Europe, have lasted for an average of 80,000 years, and interglacials, when the ice caps have retreated to approximately their present extent, tend to last for around 10,000 years.[1] What I have so far been referring to as the Ice Age was in fact the last glacial period from approximately 115,000 to 12,000 years ago. To be precise, the ice began slowly retreating around 18,000 years ago, but it was not until around 10,000 BCE that countries at the latitude of the British Isles and southern Canada were ice-free. And the subsequent rise in sea levels until about 6,000 years ago reveals that the polar ice sheets did not fully retreat to approximately their present extent until that time. During the period from the first thawing until 4000 BCE, the world's mean annual temperature rose by about 7 degrees Celsius (13 degrees Fahrenheit) and has remained relatively stable ever since (if we exclude recent climate change due to human activity).

In addition to land ice, there are also floating ice shelves like those stretching beyond the continent of Antarctica, and the ice covering the sea surrounding the North Pole. Interestingly, melting sea ice does not alter sea levels in the way melting land ice does. The mass of floating ice is the same as the mass of the water it displaces, meaning that when it melts water levels remains the same. (If you find this hard to believe, try placing an ice cube in a glass of water, marking the water level on the glass, and then checking to see where the water level is once the ice has melted.) Icebergs, however, are often breakaway sections of ice shelves, or glaciers formed from compacted snow, and consequently consist of fresh water.[2] Although the effect of the melting of such icebergs on worldwide sea levels was nominal, between 7000 and 4000 BCE their lower density caused a separate but drastic consequence for the climate of northern Europe: surprisingly, global warming caused periods of colder weather.

In many regions of the Earth, ocean currents play a significant role in climate control. For example, the British Isles and northern Europe would today be much colder if it were not for the Gulf Stream and its extension, the North Atlantic Drift. A continuous ocean current carries heated, subtropical waters of the Gulf of Mexico across the northern Atlantic to warm the sea surrounding northwest Europe. Here, the prevailing westerly winds pick up warm air from the ocean before blowing over land, assuring that the climate in this region remains temperate. If global warming should significantly increase the melting of icebergs in the North Atlantic before they have time to drift farther south, then billions of tons of fresh water would be released into the northern ocean, making the surface water less dense and unable to sink. With colder water on the surface, the prevailing winds would pick up less heat, and air temperatures in regions over which they blow would fall even as the world heated up. If it were not for the Gulf Stream, Great Britain, Ireland, and other parts of northwest Europe would be almost as cold as Alaska. A significant drop in temperatures would occur in other regions of the world if the same thing happened to ocean currents there, including Japan, Argentina, parts of China, eastern Russia, and of course Doggerland. Such melting ice can also alter or even reverse stabilizing ocean currents. Scientists can establish ancient sea temperatures by the deposits of flora and fauna found in seafloor sediment. The remains of animals and vegetation once thriving there reveal what the climate was like while they lived, and their depth within in the deposits determines how long ago they were laid down. Such research has revealed that many parts of the world were subjected to dramatic ocean current shifts and cancellations during the postglacial period between 9,000 and 6,000 years ago, precisely when the first urban cultures were emerging—such as that on North Doggerland.[3]

Archaeology has revealed many examples of early proto-civilizations being destroyed by the sudden onset of cold caused by such changes to marine currents. For example, it became cold enough in northeast China to completely wipe out early urban cultures just as they seemed poised to make significant technical advances. From the archaeological examination of the remains of ancient vegetation preserved in the soil, it is known that Heilongjiang Province in northwest China experienced a mild climate between 8,000 and 7,000 years ago. This was primarily due to the so-called Kuroshio Current bringing warm water up from the equator. During this time urban settlements, as advanced as the contemporary Chinese proto-civilization at Jiahu discussed in the previous chapter, sprang up throughout the region. But around 5000 BCE, melting icebergs in the North Pacific reversed the northern flow of the Kuroshio stream and created the Oyashio Current. This brought cold water to the area, changing the climate from warm and pleasant to almost subarctic for a time, and the ancient Heilongjiang culture abruptly ended.[4]

It may seem counterintuitive that global warming brought colder temperatures to some regions, but that is not the only oddity. We have seen how postglacial climate change brought more rainfall due to melting ice; the same phenomenon also resulted in other areas experiencing long-term droughts, turning fertile zones into arid deserts. One example is what happened to the mysterious civilization that created Göbekli Tepe, the earliest known urban culture, seemingly on the very brink of becoming a fully fledged civilization. Göbekli Tepe in southeast Turkey is a huge complex of stone structures erected around 11,500 years ago. This is an astonishing 7,000 years before the building of Stonehenge and the pyramids of Egypt. Göbekli Tepe is composed of at least 20 stone circles (4 uncovered and 16 more detected by geophysics surveys), ranging from 30 to 90 feet in diameter, and consisting of precision-cut pillars decorated with carvings of animals, humans, and various mythical creatures, more sophisticated than anything known again until the rise of the Sumer civilization millennia later. The site covers some 22 acres, although that may be just a part of the complex; archaeologists have much more of the surrounding area still to excavate. In addition, there are the foundations of rectangular dwellings serviced by an elaborate water supply system involving cisterns and irrigation channels. Dating from around 9500 BCE, at the time of writing it is by far the oldest permanent human settlement yet discovered anywhere on the planet, exhibiting a level of society and technological knowhow not seen again for thousands of years. Unlike the freestanding stone circles of the later British Isles, the Göbekli Tepe stones were rings of monoliths up to 13 feet high, set into concentric brick walls. At the center of the arrangement were a pair of much larger, 18-foot, T-shaped megaliths weighing about 10 tons. The purpose of the Göbekli Tepe complex remains a mystery, but whatever its function it must represent the achievements of a sizable proto-civilization that existed in the surrounding region, its other structures yet to be discovered.[5] But, like the Heilongjiang culture in China, it ended abruptly due to postglacial climate change. In this case it was drought, not cold, that brought about the demise. By 8000 BCE, hotter temperatures resulted in higher rainfall in the tropics, reducing the amount of water vapor held in the atmosphere. This meant that the air carried by the so-called Hadley cell—atmospheric circulation where air rises near the equator to flow poleward and descend in the subtropics—brought far less rainfall to previously humid areas such as southern Turkey, which became a parched wasteland unable to support human habitation.[6] Accordingly, around 8000 BCE Göbekli Tepe was abandoned and forgotten until its rediscovery by archaeologists in the 1990s.

Ice sheets, glaciers, and icebergs were not the only kinds of frozen water to melt during Neolithic global warming. Something else had the potential to claim far more lives than rising sea levels, higher rainfall, changing ocean currents, and disruption of atmospheric airflow combined: the melting of permafrost.

Interestingly, at the end of the Ice Age, due to sea currents bringing warm air from the tropics, the area of Doggerland enjoyed the kind of weather Britain has today. Called a temperate climate, it consisted of cool, wet winters and warm, wet summers, rarely featuring the extremes of heat or cold, drought or flooding common in other climates. However, most northern lands free of ice were still frigid wastelands. But these were beginning to thaw.

Permafrost, which would not have been found at Doggerland, is underlying ground that remains below freezing all year round, even when the summer sun warms the surface. In the Northern Hemisphere permafrost covers large areas including northern Canada, Alaska, and Siberia, known collectively as tundra. These treeless, frigid, polar deserts are inhospitable places for many life forms, yet they are ideal environments to preserve microbes, such as viruses and bacteria, in a state of dormancy for thousands or even millions of years. It was once thought that prolonged periods of freezing would destroy microbes, but recently scientists revived various species that had been buried in permafrost for thousands of years. The ability of some microorganisms to reanimate is due to both a remarkably slow metabolism and their ability to repair damaged DNA. In multicellular organisms a few cells might survive in this way, but on nowhere near the scale to enable reanimation of the entire entity, be it human, animal, or plant.[7]

Scientists have discovered various potentially deadly, contagious germs in the Arctic permafrost. For instance, viable samples of the Spanish flu virus, which killed over 50 million people between 1918 and 1920, have been extracted from the Alaskan tundra; smallpox, thought to have been eradicated throughout the world, has been found in northern Canada; and anthrax, a possible biological warfare agent, has been identified in Siberia. Today, these diseases can be controlled. There is an effective inoculation for smallpox, anthrax is caused by a bacterium that can be treated with antibiotics, and vaccines for new flu variants are manufactured every year. Also, because outbreaks of such diseases occurred comparatively recently in human history, many people have inherited natural immunity. But what happens when microorganisms have been frozen for much longer, and immunity is no longer a factor, or a virus is completely different from anything we have encountered in modern times. It was possible to create Covid-19 vaccines relatively quickly because it is a coronavirus—a family of viruses that cause illness ranging from the common cold to SARS—and scientists have been working on these for years. However, much older microorganisms may be lurking, still viable, in ancient permafrost—bacterial, viral, and fungal diseases for which we would have little or no immunity, and which are markedly different from anything previously studied.[8]

There are many illnesses that are usually little more than an inconvenience, like the common cold, and others that are seldom fatal, such as influenza, measles, chickenpox, mumps, and rubella. But they are only less malign than they might once have been because our ancestors built up resistance from prolonged exposure. Ages ago, these diseases would have been far more serious, but survivors developed antibodies to prevent such illnesses or render them less severe, passing these traits on to their descendants. Communities previously unexposed to such transmittable diseases are far more susceptible to the most severe ill effects. This is dramatically illustrated by what happened when the indigenous people of the Americas, separated from the rest of the world for thousands of years, first encountered Europeans. Colonizing Europeans deliberately killed many of them, but the vast majority were eradicated by illnesses brought by the invaders. These diseases included chickenpox, measles, influenza, and the common cold, of which a large proportion of the European population had grown immune, at least to their more severe effects. Indeed, many of those who crossed the Atlantic were carriers of such illnesses with no noticeable symptoms.[9]

In eastern North America some indigenous tribes suffered mortality rates of up to 50 percent, while others were brought close to extinction or were wiped out entirely. In Florida alone the Native American population was reduced from an estimated 700,000 in 1520 to a mere 2,000 by the year 1700. By the nineteenth century, small numbers of Europeans who ventured into the so-called Wild West brought with them diseases that caused death on an immense scale. By the time of significant European colonization of the Midwest, the Native American population had plummeted by around 90 percent. In Central America things were just as bad. When the conquistadors first arrived in 1519, the Mexican population is estimated to have been around 30 million—fifty years later, only 3 million were left alive. The same happened in the Caribbean. In the late fifteenth century, the Taino people of Hispaniola, for instance, numbered close to a million, but within fifty years of first contact with Columbus and his companions in 1492 they were virtually extinct. And in South America, the Inca Empire, which numbered around 12 million people when the Spanish arrived in 1532, was reduced by more than half by diseases like smallpox, influenza, typhus, diphtheria, chicken pox, and measles in just ten years.[10] The reverse fate did not befall the Europeans, as the Native Americans had far fewer transmittable diseases with which to infect them, their populations tending to remain within specific regions. (The same tragedies had not occurred during European colonization of various regions of the Middle East, Asia, and Africa. For centuries, populations here had extensive interaction with others, either through warfare or conquest, but particularly via trade routes linking Europe with the Middle East, Northern Africa, India, China, and the vast expanse of central Asia. Countless pathogens had long circulated across entire continents, resulting in high levels of resistance, sometimes called herd immunity, for the survivors and their descendants.)

If not reexposed to a particular contagious disease, acquired resistance diminishes over time, and after generations immunity may be lost entirely. Consequently, viable ancient pathogens able to infect humans, to which our ancestors once had immunity, if released from melted permafrost have the potential to result in deadly diseases in populations with no immunity. In 2016 an unusual heat wave thawed an ancient layer of permafrost in the Siberian tundra, releasing long dormant anthrax spores that infected dozens of people and about 2,000 reindeer. The epidemic was only contained because it occurred in the Yamal Peninsula, an extremely remote area.[11] Over the last few years, melting permafrost in Alaska has released a respiratory virus called PDV (Phocine Distemper Virus). Fatal to seals, it has virtually wiped out all the animals both on the mainland and on many Arctic islands. It may be only a matter of time before a similar disease, from which there is little natural immunity, finds its way into the human population.[12] Today, climate change is only beginning to melt lower latitude permafrost, releasing relatively recent and familiar pathogens to which we still have resistance. But as global warming continues and the tundra retreats, more ancient pathogens are sure to be awakened. Many species could face extinction. Indeed, exactly this may have occurred when primeval pathogens were released from melting permafrost following the last glacial period.

Today, about 11 percent of the global surface is underlain by permafrost, but during the last glacial period that number was far higher. At the end of what, for convenience, I will refer to as the "last Ice Age," the contemporary tundra retreated across vast regions of the planet, completely thawing permafrost over an area of at least 5 million square miles. The last Ice Age lasted for around 100,000 years, meaning that potentially deadly microbes were released from ground that had been permanently frozen for far longer than humans and animals had retained a resistance to them. Around 10,000 years ago, many animals living near or within the tundra regions suddenly became extinct, including vast herds of mammoths. It was once thought that climate change deprived the mammoths of their staple diet of flowering herbs, but that is now known to be untrue. On the contrary, the new grasslands that sprung up where there had once been sparse vegetation should have *increased* their number. In locations away from melting permafrost, where they remained in isolation—such as St. Paul Island in the Bering Sea, and Wrangel Island in the Arctic Ocean—they thrived for another 6,000 years.[13] Some scholars have suggested that mammoths were hunted to extinction by humans, but there is no archaeological evidence that Stone Age peoples were responsible.

The mammoths went extinct in North America, Scandinavia, and Siberia, but if humans were responsible for killing off these large animals, why were reindeer, elk, deer, moose, and other Arctic antelopes spared? Indeed, in 2009, Ross MacPhee, curator of the Department of Mammalogy at the American Museum of Natural History, New York—one of the world's leading experts on extinction biology and high-latitude faunas—said of the rapid disappearance of the mammoths that, "the only thing capable of causing extinctions of this type and scale was a highly lethal contagious disease."[14] Other high-latitude animals also became extinct as the tundra warmed at the end of the last Ice Age, such as the mastodon, woolly rhinoceros, dire wolf, and smilodon (often referred to as the saber-toothed tiger).[15] Many scientists believe that these too may have been wiped out by new, deadly pathogens released from the permafrost. (The same case made for the mammoth applies to the woolly rhinoceros and the mastodon, while plenty of prey remained for the smilodon and dire wolf, such as deer, elk, and reindeer.)

Direct evidence that viruses or bacteria released from melting permafrost afflicted humans is difficult to obtain. Prehistoric human remains containing identifiable vestiges of ancient microorganisms are rare, only surviving in exceptional circumstances such as where bodies were frozen or preserved in peat bogs. However, there is strong, indirect evidence from prehistoric times that an ancient disease freed from tundra permafrost *did* ravage northern and eastern Europe around 6,000 years ago.[16] Seas were still rising at this time, ice was still receding (although not to previous extents), and permafrost continued to melt in areas such as Scandinavia. Even today, northern Sweden, Norway, and Finland are tundra regions, but around 6,000 years ago the permafrost reached farther south. And it was in Sweden, about 4000 BCE, where the permafrost was still melting, that a dreadful pandemic may have begun.

Archaeologists have long been baffled by the sudden depopulation of parts of northern and eastern Europe around 4000 BCE. Some 7,500 years ago, the Trypillia culture sprang up in eastern Europe. Starting in Moldova, it quickly spread to what is now Romania, Ukraine, and Southern Poland. (It is after an archaeological site in central Ukraine that the culture is named.) One of the most advanced peoples to emerge in Europe during Neolithic times, the Trypillians practiced large-scale farming, made kiln-fired pottery, created sophisticated amulets, ornamentations, and innovative textiles, and were one of the first cultures in the world to smelt copper and domesticate horses. They also built the largest known settlements in all of Neolithic Europe, some containing over 3,000 dwellings and between 10,000 and 20,000 inhabitants. Talianki, in central Ukraine, is typical of the large Trypillian settlements that have been excavated. Occupied from around 4800 BCE, the site covered about 1,100 acres, contained approximately 2,700 structures, and is estimated to have had a population of over 15,000. Interconnected, two-story timber buildings were laid out in concentric rows, their walls and ceilings decorated with red and white designs like the patterns found on their pottery.[17] Most experts agree that the Trypillia culture was poised to become a true civilization, yet around 6,000 years ago many of these settlements were mysteriously abandoned, not to be reoccupied for several generations. Judging by the size of the much smaller Trypillian villages still occupied over the following century, population levels had abruptly plummeted. As archaeologists have unearthed no evidence of invasion, famine, or any meteorological disasters at this time, the most likely explanation is disease.

At the same time as the Trypillian settlements were being abandoned, there were dramatic drops in population levels in other cultures in northern Europe and Scandinavia, some disappearing from the archaeological record entirely. To the immediate northwest of the Trypillia culture there was the so-called Linear Pottery culture, named after the characterizing incisions on their ceramic ware. The culture spread from Hungary, through Austria and Germany, and reached the North Sea in the Netherlands. Although not as advanced as the Trypillia people, the Linear Pottery culture lived in sizable settlements of about 1,000 inhabitants, the populations of which fell significantly around 4000 BCE. Radiocarbon dating has shown that there were regular burials until approximately 6,000 years ago, when they abruptly ceased, while mass cremations occurred around the same time. For example, excavations at Elsloo in the Dutch province of Limburg revealed that a settlement of about 100 dwellings was abruptly abandoned. The remains of about forty cremated individuals were also unearthed, strongly indicating a mass disposal of bodies at the very time the settlement ceased to be occupied. Similar findings have emerged from the archaeological sites of Langweiler and Zwenkau in west and east-central Germany, and Strogen and Brunn am Gebirge in Austria.[18] As with their neighbors (the Trypillia culture), such archaeological evidence implies that an epidemic swept through the areas occupied by the Linear Pottery culture around 4000 BCE.

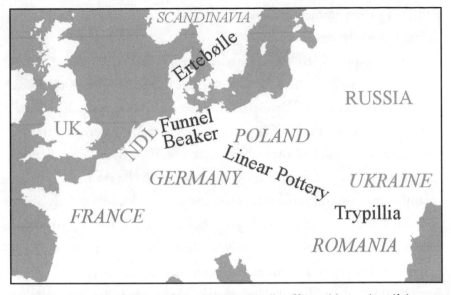

Fig. 5.1. Populations of Europe potentially affected by a dreadful pandemic of 4000 BCE.

Strikingly similar evidence is found with the contemporary Funnel Beaker culture of northern Germany, a culture named after the distinctive handle-less, funnel-shaped drinking vessels accompanying their burials. They were the first farming society in this region, and are now known to have invented wheeled carts (deduced from depictions of oxen-drawn, wheeled vehicles depicted on Funnel Beaker ceramics) seven centuries before the Sumerians supposedly invented the wheel. Numerous Funnel Beaker burial mounds were created in Schleswig-Holstein for some 300 years from the beginning of the culture around 4300 BCE, but then none were created for the following century, until a new influx of Funnel Beaker people arrived from Poland around 3900 BCE. This is known from archaeological sites like those at Rastorf, Wangels, and Wolkenwehe in Schleswig-Holstein.[19] Clearly, something seems to have wiped out the early Funnel Beaker peoples in north Germany. Because a plague of some kind also appears to have been affecting the contemporary Trypillia culture to their immediate south at precisely this same time, an epidemic is a likely explanation.

Another people to the immediate north of Schleswig-Holstein disappears entirely from the archaeological record around 4000 BCE: the Ertebølle culture of Denmark and Sweden. The Ertebølle culture, so dubbed after a village of that name in Denmark where its remains were first excavated, had thrived from around 5300 BCE. They derived their living primarily from fishing, not only from the sea but also from inland rivers, meaning that their settlements were located chiefly along coastlines and riverbanks. Although they manufactured sophisticated ceramics, they were technologically less advanced than their southern neighbors. They used dugout canoes, and their homes were constructed from light wood and brush. Nonetheless, their cemeteries, located near settlements, appear to have been well-tended and used over long periods of time. High-status individuals, most likely the ruling elite and priesthood, were interred in chambered cairns (earthen mounds placed over compartments made from an arrangement of stone blocks—basically tombs as opposed to graves). Radiocarbon dating has found no evidence of any further cairn burials from around 4000 BCE, while pottery dating* has indicated that settlements abruptly ceased to be occupied at the same time.[20] Significantly, mass graves containing up to 100 individuals have been found at archaeological sites throughout the Ertebølle region—such as at Vigsor, Appenaes, and Vejlø Skov in Denmark, and Skateholm and Gränsstigen in southern Sweden—all seemingly dating to the same time, around 4000 BCE. All this clearly indicates that a dreadful disaster swept the area some 6,000 years ago.

---

*The dating of fired clay ceramics, like bricks, tiles, and pottery, relies on the fact that they gradually chemically combine with water after the firing process, which occurs at a predictable rate. By measuring the mass of a sample of ceramic and then heating it to remove the water, the measured resultant mass enables a highly accurate determination of the time the item was made.

So, four separate cultures within a large region of northeastern and central Europe all experienced either an abrupt plummet or complete disappearance of population, sudden abandonment of settlements, and the simultaneous mass disposal of human bodies—all at the same time. As examination of vegetation remains in the relevant soil strata of the area dating from the time of the event reveals no evidence of crop failures, and as there is no evidence from ring analysis of trees preserved in peat bogs concerning abrupt climate disruption, famine can be ruled out. Neither are there any indications of a sudden influx of newcomers to the region, ruling out invasion or large-scale migration.[21] An epidemic of some kind is by far the most feasible scenario: actually, a *pandemic*—an epidemic spread over multiple countries. These cultures were all connected both geographically and by trade. (Pottery specifically associated with adjacent cultures has been found mixed with the native ceramics throughout these regions.) A transmissible infection could indeed have spread throughout the entire region.

As noted, proving that such a pandemic occurred is difficult. Nevertheless, an excavation of a 6,000-year-old mass grave at Frälsegården in Falbygden, in western Sweden, in the early years of the twenty-first century produced the first evidence that a deadly and highly contagious disease did indeed sweep Scandinavia around 4000 BCE. The burial site contained some 78 individuals who seem to have been interred simultaneously, some in a remarkable state of preservation, sufficient to extract viable DNA from microorganisms. And in 2015, scientific analysis revealed the cause of death: a variant of the bacterium *Yersinia pestis,* the germ suspected to have caused the Black Death,* which between 1347 and 1351

---

*The variant of *Yersinia pestis* the researchers discovered was not actually the kind that caused the Black Death—bubonic plague—but its nastier cousin, pneumonic plague. Bubonic plague spreads via bites from fleas carried by rodents; pneumonic plague directly infects the lungs and spreads from person to person through saliva droplets, like influenza.

is estimated to have killed as many as 100 million people across Europe, or more than 50 percent of the population.[22] Since 2015 the presence of *Yersinia pestis* has been found in more human remains from this period in the Ertebølle, Trypillia, Linear Pottery, and Funnel Beaker cultures, all suggesting that the plague may indeed have been responsible for the decimation of these cultures. It is difficult to determine where it started, but the consensus is that it moved southward, beginning in what is now Sweden, in what had then been tundra to the north of Falbygden.[23] It is therefore quite possible that melting permafrost caused the release of dormant microbes that all but wiped out some of the earliest urban cultures in Europe.

Now that we are familiar with the terrible effects that global warming had on the world after the last Ice Age, and the types of devastation inflicted on early proto-civilizations, we are ready to return to the British Isles.

6

The Mysteries of the Megalithic Culture

······················

Postulating Its Origins

Before examining the possibility that a forgotten culture existed on a lost land to the north of the British Isles over six millennia ago, we should remind ourselves of the postglacial climate change events affecting Neolithic peoples up until the time the Bay of Firth megalithic complex began to submerge.

20,000 BCE. Height of last Ice Age. So much of the world's water was tied up in ice that global sea levels were an astonishing 400 feet lower than today. Average world temperature was some 5 degrees Celsius (10 degrees Fahrenheit) lower than in modern times.

20,000–12,000 BCE: Temperatures increased, ice melted, and the glaciers and vast ice sheets began to retreat. Sea levels rose by approximately 140 feet.

10,000–7000 BCE. The emergence of new land previously under ice led to significant migrations of human populations, and the beginning of farming and village settlements, a period known as the early Neolithic. By then, sea levels had risen to about 190 feet lower than today.

7000–4000 BCE. The mid-Neolithic, when advances in the cultivation of crops and domestication of animals led to larger settlements: the so-called "first cities" or urbian settlements, such as Plovdiv in Bulgaria, Jiahu in China, and Jericho in Palestine. By 7000 BCE sea levels had risen to some 100 feet lower than today.

6500 BCE. The Greenland Slide caused a megatsunami that overwhelmed Majuán Isle off the coast of Morocco—the possible origin of the Atlantis legend.

6300 BCE. Sea levels had risen to about 60 feet lower than today. By now, in various parts of the world, humanity had entered an age of ceramics and sophisticated brickmaking, and large settlements of more than 1,000 inhabitants had been established.

6200 BCE. Storegga Slides on the coast of Norway resulted in a megatsunami overtaking the coast of North America.

6000 BCE. Sea 50 feet lower than today.

5700 BCE. Chinese Peiligang culture flooded.

5500 BCE. Final submergence of the Indus Shelf, off the present mouth of the Indus River in Pakistan.

5500 BCE. Gulf Oasis in Mesopotamia submerged.

5500 BCE. Delta Shelf submerged off the coast of Egypt.

5500 BCE. Black Sea Flood—possible origin of the biblical Noah story.

5000 BCE. Submergence of the Palk Strait land bridge between southern India and Sri Lanka—candidate for a historical Lemuria.

5000–4000 BCE. The Mokaya coastal towns of western Central America submerged as seas rose by around 30 feet—possible origin of the Mu legend.

4000 BCE. Pandemic sweeps through the Ertebølle, Linear Pottery, Funnel Beaker, and Trypillia cultures of Scandinavia, the Netherlands, Germany, Poland, Romania, Moldova, and Ukraine.

4000 BCE. The late Neolithic. Sea levels only about 12 feet lower than today. The Firth Circle megalithic complex off the coast of the Orkney Islands begins to submerge.

The megalithic complex that now lies on the seabed, 12 feet below the surface in the Bay of Firth off the Orkney Islands, began sinking around 4000 BCE. We therefore know that it can be no less than 6,000 years old, created at least a millennium before any known stone circles were erected in the mainland British Isles. Its discovery demonstrates first that the Megalithic culture in Great Britain and Ireland was much older than previously thought, and second that the submerged circle, close to shore, meant that around 4000 BCE the Orkney Islands had a more extensive coastline that might have contained further megalithic monuments. Exciting notions in their own right! However, from what geologists have determined, there might have been an entire, much

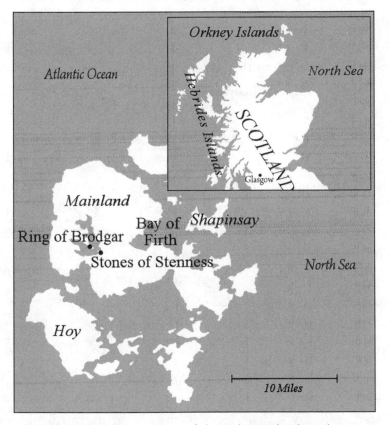

Fig. 6.1. The location of the Orkney Islands and
the sites of the Brodgar, Stenness, and Bay of Firth stone circles.

earlier Megalithic civilization previously existing on what was extensive land far to the northeast of the Orkney Islands. Bathymetric analysis—the study of underwater landscapes—has revealed that 7,000 years ago a large island certainly existed there.

Extending 50 miles north and 40 miles east of the present Orkney Islands, an area approximately the size of Rhode Island, the now-sunken island is officially called North Doggerland, although from here forward I shall be referring to it by the more lyrical Fairland, after the modern Fair Isle shipping area in which it was located. Doggerland had been another, larger such island to the east of England named after the Dogger shipping area, which undersea surveys suggest became submerged by rising sea levels by 7000 BCE.[1] Until recently, scientists reasoned that Fairland disappeared around the same time. However, it is now known that a crucial type of geological activity called isostatic adjustment had been overlooked. During the last Ice Age, compacted ice sheets more than two miles thick had covered northern Britain, and their massive weight, pushing down over a period of 100,000 years, crushed the land beneath, depressing it by hundreds of feet. Once the ice retreated, the northern British Isles slowly began to rise, countering the effect of rising sea levels. Consequently, Fairland was not submerged until much later than Doggerland.[2] Indeed, parts of it are now thought to have remained above sea level until the fifth millennium BCE—the time that the Bay of Firth megalithic complex is thought to have been created. Could Fairland have been where the Megalithic culture originated? Might the monuments found on the seabed off the Orkney Islands be evidence of a civilization that once existed on Fairland, the legendary Tu-lay from where it was said the first stone circle builders had come?

Let's remind ourselves of what was discovered on the seabed to the east of the Orkneys' Mainland Isle in 2011. The team, led by archaeologists Caroline Wickham-Jones of the University of Aberdeen and Richard Bates from the Department of Earth and Environmental

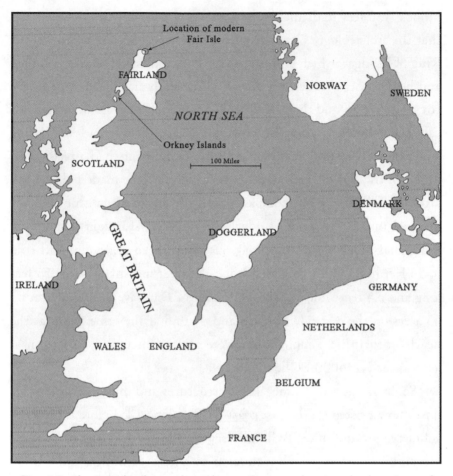

Fig. 6.2. The British Isles and northwest Europe, showing the locations of prehistoric Doggerland and Fairland, as well as the modern Orkney Islands and Fair Isle.

Sciences at the University of St. Andrews, discovered a submerged circular embankment about 450 feet in diameter and, within it, the remains of a stone circle consisting of six fallen monoliths, each about 15 feet long, lying on the seabed. When their locations in relation to one another were taken into consideration, they appeared to have been the remains of a stone circle about 350 feet that may originally have consisted of some 50 to 60 monoliths. Additionally, about 450 feet southwest of the circle there appeared to be the remains of an artificial hillock, 130 feet in diameter and some 10 feet high. All this suggested that the archaeologists had discovered a very similar monument to the Ring of Brodgar, which still exists on Mainland Isle. The size, number, and height of the stones, the surrounding ditch and embankment, the circle's diameter, and the nearby artificial hillock were all almost identical. The submerged complex was some 12 feet below sea level, dating it to at least 4000 BCE. More Neolithic monuments had already been found in the Bay of Firth, two years earlier, but not made public until after the full survey was completed and the entire megalithic complex mapped in 2011. Previous underwater surveys had identified several individual fallen stones that may once have been erect monoliths up to 15 feet high, and a collapsed stone chamber measuring some 25 feet long and 6.5 feet wide, off the west coast of Damsay, an islet of around 45 acres on the east side of Mainland. Found at the same depth as the nearby megalithic complex, they were also estimated to date from at least as early as 4000 BCE.[3]

So, in summary, the megalithic structures and monuments that we now know existed on the east coast of Mainland Isle before it began to submerge around 4000 BCE are very similar to the Ring of Brodgar megalithic complex, which is thought to have been built about 6 miles to the west centuries later. Along with what appear to have been individual, free-standing monoliths like those still found dotted around the Orkney landscape, there were the remains of a stone chamber identical to the so-called chambered tombs that were later built on the Orkneys throughout the fourth millennium BCE. This all means that what we now call the Megalithic culture, which eventually spread throughout the entire British Isles, was already in existence on the Orkney Islands at least 6,000 years ago—1,000 years before it was adopted elsewhere. In short, the culture was at least a millennium older than previously thought.

Before continuing, we should familiarize ourselves with what exactly the Megalithic culture was. Best known for building Stonehenge, it quickly spread throughout the British Isles around 3000 BCE, erecting vast numbers of stone and earthen monuments. The stone circles, for which the culture is renowned, generally measured from approximately 20 to 100 feet in diameter and consisted of between 10 and 30 shaped standing stones ranging from 3 to 15 feet high. About 1,100 of these rings still exist in various states of preservation, but originally there must have been many thousands. Additionally, there were the very much larger stone circles with diameters up to an astonishing 1,000 feet, consisting of over 100 stones, some weighing as much as 40 tons.

Many of these stone circles, both large and small, had a single monolith standing some distance outside the main ring—known as a "king stone"—aligned to the rising or setting of the sun at important

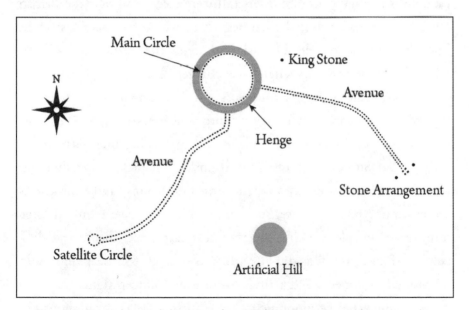

Fig. 6.3. Typical megalithic complex. With main stone circles measuring between 100 and 1,000 feet in diameter, and surrounded by a ditch and embankment, such complexes often included satellite rings and other arrangements of megaliths at the end of standing stone or earthen avenues, as well as outlier monoliths and artificial hills.

times of the year, such as the midsummer and midwinter solstice (the longest and shortest days of the year).

The larger stone circles, such as Avebury, Stonehenge, and the Ring of Brodgar, also had other arrangements of standing stones within them—like smaller circles, single monoliths, and horseshoe-shaped stone arrangements known as coves—and were often adjoined by avenues of parallel monoliths, sometimes running for miles, as well as smaller satellite stone circles. They were generally surrounded by a ringed earthwork consisting of deep ditches and a high embankment called a henge and nearby artificial hills. It seems that these megalithic complexes, which include the sizable stone circle and these other features, were created near larger, more prosperous settlements, while the smaller circles were close to lesser villages.

In addition to stone circles, thousands of freestanding, solitary monoliths averaging around 6 feet tall were erected all over the British Isles. Sometimes separated by miles, these were often set in straight lines that ran for considerable distances across the landscape, occasionally linking separate stone circles (see chapter 7).

The creation of these monuments were often mammoth undertakings for a Neolithic people digging into solid bedrock, building huge earthworks, quarrying stone, and intricately shaping monoliths using nothing but Stone Age tools: animal antlers for picks, oxen shoulder blades for shovels, stone axes for hacking and shaping, and flint knives for cutting. And, of course, such projects would have required large numbers of people working together to quarry, cut, shape, and drag colossal stones as well as dig huge ditches over 40 feet deep and build 40-foot embankments and artificial hills over 100 feet high.[4]

As these types of monuments were all so similar throughout the British Isles, clearly during the third millennium BCE the inhabitants of these islands were a unified culture—something close to a civilization, though they had no roads, beasts of burden, or significant metallurgy, nor the complex cities that we find with their contemporary civilizations in Egypt, Sumer, and the Indus Valley. Despite this, they were, in fact, one of the most complex urbian cultures of the Neolithic era anywhere in the world. Although their smaller communities were villages of about 100 inhabitants, the larger settlements were certainly what we have been calling "early cities." Built close to the larger megalithic complexes, they accommodated well over 5,000 people, such as at Durrington Walls near Stonehenge.

Domestic dwellings* were basically single-roomed, circular, wickerwork constructions fashioned from tree branches, with dried-mud walls and thatched roofs. Dwellings in more forested areas were rectangular log structures divided into two or more chambers with roofs overlaid with turf, not dissimilar to the simple cabins of the early European pioneers in the American West. None of these have left traces to be seen today, but they have been identified by archaeologists using geophysics equipment to detect signs of ancient postholes in the ground, their age determined by the radiocarbon dating of decomposed timber remains in the soil.[5]

Another common feature of the period was a specific type of burial structure called a passage tomb, typically a ditch and embankment surrounding a circular mound, inside of which were stone-lined chambers accessed by a long passageway. Seven such tombs still survive on the Orkney Islands, the largest of which is known as Maeshowe. Standing about half a mile to the east of the Stones of Stenness, its mound is 115 feet in diameter and rises to a height of 24 feet. Its low entrance passage

---

*For those who wish to see how the people of the era lived, five Neolithic houses, complete with replica pottery, tools, simple wooden furnishings, and various artifacts, have been reconstructed outside the visitor center at Stonehenge. They are of the wickerwork frame type, with the interior walls whitewashed with ground chalk, a design tactic thought to not only make the dwellings brighter but also to reflect warmth from the fire. The outside walls are also whitewashed to reflect the heat of sunlight in the summertime.[6] On certain occasions reenactors dress up in Neolithic style and perform ancient daily activities in and around the dwellings.

is 3 feet high and about 36 feet long, leading to a 12-foot-high square chamber, measuring about 15 feet on each side. Some of the larger stones used to create Maeshowe weigh over 3 tons. The central chamber is constructed of flat stone slabs, many traversing the entire sides of the chamber, with the top part of the walls constructed of overlapping slabs to create a beehive-shaped roof. In each corner is a cleverly designed buttress to support the ceiling, each made from stacked stones, together with a large standing stone about 8 feet high. Three side chambers, or cells, averaging about 6 feet by 5 feet and about 3 feet high, are accessed by 2.5-foot-square entrances, each built halfway along the side and rear walls, some 2 feet above the ground. Today, a large stone, thought to have been used to seal the chambers, lies on the floor outside each of these cells.[7] Throughout the British Isles, tombs built to a similar design were a common feature of the early Megalithic era; some were smaller, such as Bryn Celli Ddu on the Isle of Anglesey off the north coast of Wales, while others were truly huge, like Newgrange in Ireland. Lying

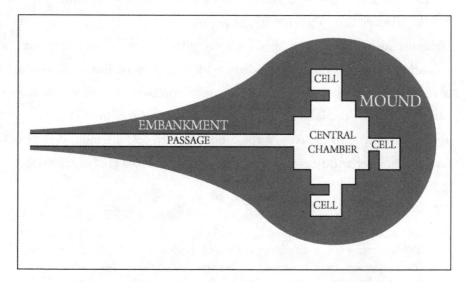

Fig. 6.4. Characteristic layout of a passage tomb, such as
Maeshowe on the Orkney Islands, with the entrance passage aligned
to the sunrise or sunset on the midsummer or midwinter solstice.

5 miles west of the town of Drogheda in County Meath on Ireland's eastern coast, its central mound is about 250 feet across and 40 feet high—by far the largest passage tomb in the British Isles—and its internal features include a scaled-up version of Maeshowe and other such tombs. An interesting aspect of these passage tombs is that, like the king stones at stone circles, the long straight passageways were often aligned to the midwinter or midsummer sunset or sunrise, so that the sun's rays would light up the central chamber at that specific time of the year.[8]

The Megalithic culture was at its height in the British Isles between 3000 and 2500 BCE, but astonishingly it continued right through a series of large-scale migrations to the British Isles from continental Europe. Here is a list of the influx of new cultures that migrated to Britain and Ireland for over 2,000 years.

C. 2500 BCE: The Beaker people from the Netherlands, named after a distinctive type of bell-shaped pottery vessel, or "beaker," found in their graves.[9]

C. 2000 BCE: The Wessex culture from Belgium, named after the region of south-central England where their remains were first identified, who brought the early Bronze Age to the British Isles.[10]

C. 1000 BCE: The Urnfield culture from Germany—named after their practice of placing the cremated ashes of their dead in pottery urns, which they buried in cemeteries or "fields"—who brought with them all the benefits of the late Bronze Age to Great Britain and Ireland.[11]

C. 700 BCE: The Iron Age Hallstatt culture from Austria, named after a site near Salzburg where a huge cemetery of the period was excavated during the nineteenth century.[12]

Throughout this entire period, up until the Roman invasion of the British Isles in the mid-first century CE, megalithic monuments continued to be built, used, and repaired. For one reason or another the Megalithic culture, or at least primary aspects of it, continued to hold sway in mainland Britain for 3,000 years, and in Ireland—which was unconquered by the Romans—for another five centuries, until its conversion to Christianity.[13] None of these cultures that inhabited the British Isles before the Roman invasion of the first century CE had their own form of writing, so we have no native written records from the Megalithic period. How, therefore, are today's researchers able to date and reconstruct events of this literally *prehistoric* era?

One of the most significant methods of determining the age of ancient remains is radiocarbon dating. All living things—fauna or flora—absorb an isotope of carbon called carbon-14. Once an organism dies, the intake ceases. Thereafter, the carbon-14 decays, or transforms, into a different isotope, nitrogen-14; hence the amount of carbon-14 decreases over time at a specific, known rate. By scientifically measuring the amount of carbon-14 still present in an organic sample, archaeologists can determine how long ago an organism died. The problem is, of course, that stones are not organic remains. It's true that many rocks incorporate fossils that were once living things, but fossils are so old that they have been petrified—literally turned to stone—by geological processes, and cannot be radiocarbon dated. As most of the megalithic monuments, as their name suggests, are made of stone, how can their ages be determined? The answer lies with organic remains found beneath monoliths. The bottoms of the pits that were dug to hold the stones were lined with broken animal bones, probably to prevent them from sinking farther into the earth, and bone is organic and can be radiocarbon dated. Of course, the results will relate to when the animals died, but it's a reasonable assumption that this was roughly the same time the stones were erected. A similar technique can be used to date earthworks, mounds, and pits that were dug and later filled in, by dating organic remains found in the soil.[14]

Plate 1. The Neolithic underground settlement of Skara Brae on the Orkney Islands. Built around 3100 BCE, it was completely covered by sand during a freak storm around 2500 BCE, preserving it almost intact. (Photography by Deborah Cartwright)

Plate 2. Rooms of homes over 5,000 years old, complete with prehistoric shelving, beds, and hearths, still survive at Skara Brae on the Orkney Islands. (Photography by Deborah Cartwright)

Plate 11. The Ring of Brodgar on the Orkney Islands appears to be a copy of an earlier stone circle, at least 6,000 years old, found on the seabed of the Bay of Firth. *(Photography by Deborah Cartwright)*

Plate 12. Mysterious alignments of megalithic standing stones can be found all over the British Isles. *(Photography by Deborah Cartwright)*

Plate 13. Long avenues of monoliths, such as this one at the Avebury megalithic complex, often join larger stone circles to smaller, satellite stone rings miles away. (Photography by Deborah Cartwright)

Plate 14. A circular earthwork comprising a ditch and embankment, known as a henge, usually surrounds the larger stone circles. (Photography by Deborah Cartwright)

Plate 15. The Stones of Stenness on the Orkney Islands, the oldest megalithic stone circle still to survive on dry land. (Photography by Deborah Cartwright)

Plate 16. *The Rudston Monolith now stands in a medieval churchyard in Yorkshire. At 25 feet high, it is the tallest megalith in Britain. Thousands of these solitary standing stones still survive from the Megalithic age.*
(Photography by Deborah Cartwright)

Plate 17. *The thousands of stone circles that covered the British Isles ranged from around 20 feet in diameter to up to 1,000 feet. The Ring of Brodgar in the Orkney Islands is one of the oldest and largest. (Photography by Deborah Cartwright)*

Plate 18. *The enigmatic henge earthworks were built with the ditch on the inside, the wrong way around, for defensive purposes. This henge at Avebury stone circles is over 60 feet from top to bottom. (Photography by Deborah Cartwright)*

Plate 19. *The megaliths of some stone circles were truly huge. This one at Avebury weighs over 100 tons. (Photography by Deborah Cartwright)*

Plate 20. *The famous Heel Stone at Stonehenge, lying some distance outside the stone circle, over which the midsummer sun rises as viewed from the center of the ring. (Photography by Deborah Cartwright)*

Plate 21. *The Bridestones box tomb in central England. Such tombs seem to have been reserved for an elite caste of healers, as the residue of ancient pharmaceutical remedies have been found on pottery discovered in them. (Photography by Deborah Cartwright)*

Plate 22. *Maeshowe mound on the Orkney Islands is one of the many passage tombs that typified the birth of the Megalithic age. (Photography by Deborah Cartwright)*

Plate 23. Thousands of megalithic stone circles were erected throughout the British Isles from around 5,000 years ago, such as the Rollright Stones in the county of Oxfordshire. (Photography by Deborah Cartwright)

Plate 24. The Dwarfie Stane on Hoy Island of the Orkneys, a carved-out chambered tomb around 6,000 years old, may be one of the first burial sites in the British Isles after North Doggerland finally sank beneath the waves. (Photography by Deborah Cartwright)

Plate 25. Many stone circles, whatever their size, tend to have a so-called king stone placed some distance outside them to align with the sunrise or sunset on the solstices, as seen from the center of the ring. (Photography by Deborah Cartwright)

Another scientific procedure to determine the age of ancient finds is ceramic dating. For some years scientists have been able to date ceramic material employing a process called thermoluminescence. When pottery is fired it undergoes a change in crystalline structure that alters over time and can be measured to determine how long ago the item was made. However, thermoluminescence dating is only accurate to a limited extent: low levels of radiation from certain types of rocks or exposure to ultraviolet rays from sunlight, for example, can contaminate the sample and render testing unreliable. Recently, however, a new and far more accurate technique has been developed to date pottery. Called rehydroxylation dating, it measures how much water pottery has absorbed since the time it was fired.[15]

There is also soil stratification. If an archaeological find is still in situ, the soil strata in which it is found can be dated by another scientific procedure, the scientific analysis of the remains of microscopic organisms such as pollen grains. This, together with geophysics equipment—such as ground-penetrating radar used to produce computer-generated images of what lies buried before any invasive excavation is necessary—makes it possible to determine where holes were dug and later refilled, even in the remote past. (Soil strata get all jumbled up when holes are dug, and geophysics reveals where the ground has been disturbed.) Such procedures show where wooden posts for such features as buildings had been set, where graves were dug, and where stones had once been erected before later being moved. And, once located, the soil strata around the disturbed hole or pit can be dated, revealing how long ago such structures were built and ground disturbances were created. And the type, depth, arrangement, and so forth of such tell-tale disturbances in the ground can reveal what kind and size of structures had been erected.[16] (Radiocarbon dating was primarily employed to fix a date for the Bay of Firth complex, as the other techniques are problematic and difficult underwater.)

The Megalithic people were in many ways a true civilization. They enjoyed a cultural consistency with sophisticated achievements—types of monuments, buildings, ceramics, customs, textiles, and so forth—which stretched throughout the entire British Isles. It was, in fact, one of the most advanced cultures of its time. Remember, the more developed civilizations of Sumer, Egypt, and the Indus Valley did not arise until about 700 years after the Megalithic culture began in the British Isles. But unlike most ancient civilizations, there is a complete lack of evidence as to how it developed. The expertise to quarry, shape, move, and erect enormous standing stones, the organizational skills needed to coordinate huge numbers of workers over long periods of time, and the evolution of highly sophisticated ceramics would have taken hundreds of years of progression. Yet—astonishingly—the Megalithic culture, when it first appeared in the Orkney Islands, was fully developed. All the accomplishments we have just listed had already been achieved. Until recently, after scientific methods dated the Stones of Stenness to around 3100 BCE, it was considered the oldest known stone circle. But now we know, from the discoveries on the seabed of the Bay of Firth, that a huge stone circle and megalithic complex, as advanced as anything found anywhere in the British Isles, already existed on the Orkneys by 4000 BCE. It seems that a fully formed Megalithic culture already existed on the Orkney Islands 6,000 years ago. In fact, it must have been considerably older. Yet, extraordinarily, there is no evidence of its previous existence or development on the Orkney Islands or anywhere else in the British Isles before this time. So, where did the Megalithic culture originate?

Some scholars have speculated that the Megalithic culture may have begun in Brittany in northern France. However, although a stone monument-building culture existed here in Neolithic times, its monuments were very different from those in the British Isles. The inhabitants of Brittany did erect solitary stones, and groups of standing stones, but these were in rows, not circles. In fact, there were no stone circles, megalithic complexes, or henge monuments anything like those in the British Isles anywhere in northern France. Furthermore, the ancient people of Brittany had a completely different type of pottery from anything found in Great Britain or Ireland.[17]

As for the other contemporary coastal regions of northern Europe, there are no ceramics, tombs, monuments, stone circles, earthworks, or anything like those found in the early Megalithic British Isles in Belgium, the Netherlands, Germany, or indeed anywhere else in the world. Although various exotic ideas have been proposed, such as seafaring migrants from the Mediterranean or the Middle East, perhaps the early Egyptians or Sumerians, the kind of dwellings, building techniques, ceramic ware, and monuments found on the Orkney Islands and subsequently in the rest of the British Isles bear little similarity to anything from that contemporary part of the world. Scandinavia is about 300 miles east of the British Isles, and as such it has been suggested as an original homeland of the Megalithic culture. However, nothing like it has been found in Denmark, Norway, or Sweden. In fact, like the contemporary peoples of the mainland British Isles around 4000 BCE, the Scandinavians were chiefly a hunter-gatherer people, still in the pre-agricultural Mesolithic Age.[18]

The only possibility left open to us seems that the Megalithic culture stemmed from some lost civilization. And that civilization, if the peoples of the ancient British Isles are to be believed, was Tu-lay—perhaps North Doggerland, the geographically known sunken island, which I am, for convenience, referring to as Fairland.

7

Stone Circles, Earthworks, and Standing Stones

....

Characteristics of the Monuments of the British Isles

Although the underwater contours of the North Sea have been thoroughly charted, no marine survey capable of identifying vestiges of a sunken civilization on the seabed has yet been conducted. (The Bay of Firth survey was only a study of what had once been the coast of the Orkney Islands, not the seabed of the North Sea where Fairland had been.) Nevertheless, indirect evidence does exist that such a civilization once existed—for instance, what may well have been Fairland's legacy: the Megalithic culture of the British Isles. If the Megalithic people did indeed inherit their culture from a lost civilization on Fairland, what we know of *them* might throw light on their predecessors.

The kind of monuments the Megalithic people left behind are pretty much the same throughout the British Isles, implying that they were essentially a single civilization (recall chapter 6). Nonetheless, that civilization seems to have been divided up into separate, autonomous tribal regions. Although there appears to have been no central administration, there does seem to have been a single, cohesive priesthood fraternity. The Megalithic British Isles would therefore perhaps have had something in common with early Dark Age England, which was divided into self-governing kingdoms who all revered the same religion (in their case, Roman Catholicism). Despite this similarity, unlike the Anglo-Saxon kingdoms who were forever feuding with one another, there is no evidence that there was any significant infighting between the tribal regions of the Megalithic British Isles. Even the migrants we met in the last chapter—the Beaker people, the Wessex culture, and others—seemed to have peacefully coexisted both with each other and the native Britons. Archaeology has found no evidence of defenses erected around settlements, and no human remains have been unearthed exhibiting the kind of injuries sustained in battle. On the contrary, the native Neolithic population and the newcomers seem to have lived and worked harmoniously together while at the same time retaining their cultural identities.[1]

Individual burial customs, for instance, remained unchanged. Archaeological excavations in and around Durrington Walls, the largest known contemporary settlement in Britain, for example, have revealed that different types of cultural burials occurred side by side for centuries, even as these ethnic groups were all involved in the continued building of stone circles. It was only around 1000 BCE, after the climate turned colder, that the first fortified settlements were built. So, for at least 2,000 years, the Megalithic culture (which included the migrants who merged with it) was one of the most long-lasting and peaceful civilizations in the world.[2]

Each tribal area seems to have had a similar array of monuments: a megalithic complex consisting of a large stone circle and other features, such as stone avenues, accompanying earthworks, and accompanying rings of stones, located near the territory's largest settlement; several smaller stone circles near lesser communities; and individual freestanding monoliths dotted throughout the region. The megalithic

complexes differed in size, but had many features in common. The largest we know of was Avebury in southern England. With a diameter of
over 1,000 feet, its primary stone circle originally consisted of about
100 stones, ranging from 9 to 20 feet high, with some weighing as much
as 40 tons. A common feature of these large stone circles surrounded it: a
circular ditch and embankment called a henge (from where Stonehenge
gets its name). At Avebury, the embankment is about 20 feet high and
40 feet thick, and the ditch is about 30 feet deep and 60 feet wide.
(Before centuries of erosion, they would have been much deeper and
larger constructs.) Intriguingly, as at other megalithic complexes, the
ditch was inside the embankment, indicating that the earthwork was
not created for defensive reasons. Such large henge circles usually had
so-called avenues leading from them—parallel rows of stones and/or
embankments that led sometimes for over a mile across the countryside
to end in a further arrangement of monoliths or a smaller stone circle
known as a satellite ring. At Avebury, an 80-foot-wide avenue of parallel monoliths was added to the southeast of the circle. Referred to as
the West Kennet Avenue, it originally consisted of about 100 pairs of
stones spaced at intervals of about 50 feet, and ran for about one and
a half miles. Twenty-seven stones, between 4 and 13 feet high, remain
standing for the first half mile of the avenue, the remainder having been
removed when the village of West Kennet and its surrounding roads
were built in the eighteenth century. The avenue ends at nearby Overton
Hill, where it adjoins what was once a smaller stone circle, known as the
Sanctuary, approximately 130 feet in diameter and consisting of about
40 stones. The Sanctuary stones have long since vanished, but today
concrete blocks mark where archaeologists determine their positions to
have been. In the year 2000, excavations and geophysical surveys conducted by the University of Southampton revealed evidence of parallel
rows of holes that once contained standing stones in a similar pattern
to the West Kennet Avenue. This second avenue of stones, called the

Fig. 7.1. Some of the larger stone circles and megalithic complexes of the British Isles.

Beckhampton Avenue, extended from the southwest side of the main circle, but only one of its monoliths still survives. It is thought to have followed a curved route for about a mile, ending in an arrangement of four huge megaliths that were recorded in the eighteenth century as the Longstone Cove. Only one of the Longstone Cove monoliths survives. Going by the name Adam, it weighs an estimated 62 tons.

(Nearby there is also a stone called Eve, the only surviving stone from the Beckhampton Avenue.)[3]

These huge megalithic complexes often included artificial hills. Three-quarters of a mile south of the main circle at Avebury, pretty much midway between the ends of the stone avenues, stands Silbury Hill. At about 130 feet high and covering some 5 acres, it is the largest artificial mound in the British Isles. Archaeologists have estimated that it would have taken around four million hours of work to build from over half a million tons of material, mainly solid chalk hacked from the surrounding land. Astonishingly, although it has been both thoroughly excavated and exhaustively scanned with geophysics equipment, there is no indication that any chambers or burials ever existed within.[4] The same is found at such artificial hills that accompany other large stone circles, such as Gop Cairn in the county of Flintshire in northern Wales. The second-largest of these megalithic artificial hills, it is a 40-foot-high mound, over 300 feet wide, standing about half a mile northwest of the village of Trelawnyd, where it is believed a megalithic stone circle complex once existed before being obliterated when the village was built during the Middle Ages. Just as with Silbury Hill, archaeologists have found the hillock has no internal structures or burials.

A primary circle, surrounding henge, avenues, satellite stone circles, and artificial hills are common features for megalithic complexes, although the centers of the primary circles seem originally to have been devoid of stones. Around 2500 BCE, however, throughout the British Isles new features were erected within these large stone circles, perhaps to add local prestige to the monuments. Unlike the basic layout of the complexes, these internal monuments tend to differ significantly from one another. At Avebury, geophysics and subsequent excavations have revealed that two further stone circles were created within the main ring, one to the north and one to the south. Approximately the same size and measuring well over 300 feet in diameter, they each consisted of about 30 stones up to 10 feet tall. Today, only four and five stones survive, respectively, from these northern and southern inner circles. While the north circle had three huge stones known as the Cove at its center, two of which still survive, the south circle had a 100-foot-square arrangement of monoliths surrounding what is estimated to have been a huge, 20-foot-tall obelisk. The Avebury complex seems to have been the principal ceremonial site for a tribe whose capital was at Windmill Hill, a Neolithic settlement of about 21 acres located about a mile northwest of the main stone circle.[5] The better known, but considerably smaller, megalithic complex of Stonehenge lies about 17 miles to the south of Avebury and seems to have been the equivalent site for a tribe whose capital was at Durrington Walls, a Neolithic settlement 2 miles northeast of the world-famous monument.[6]

Surprisingly, the Stonehenge we see today—created around 2500 BCE—was not the original stone circle on the site. There is a ring of depressions in the ground around 280 feet in diameter that completely encircles the main monument. Known as the Aubrey Holes (after a seventeenth-century antiquarian who first recorded them) they are thought to mark the locations of the original stones erected around 3000 BCE. Modern geophysics has determined that these are the remains of 56 pits, each between 3 and 4 feet wide and dug to a depth of about 3 feet, which—because of crushed rubble excavated from the bottom of the holes, obviously caused by something heavy—are thought to have been pits dug to hold monoliths. Based on the principle that about a third of a monolith needed to be implanted in the ground to keep it standing, it is estimated that the Aubrey Holes delineate a now vanished stone circle consisting of 56 stones, approximately 6 feet high, 3.5 feet wide, and 2.5 feet thick. This original monument was surrounded by a henge earthwork over 300 feet in diameter, much eroded today. Stonehenge also had an avenue leading to a smaller stone circle. It once consisted of a pair of parallel banks, originally about 6 feet high and 20 feet wide, set about

70 feet apart, with a ditch outside them, which followed a bending trajectory for nearly 2 miles to the east of the stone circle. Geophysics surveys conducted in the 1980s indicated that uniformly spaced standing stones ran along these embankments—about 50 in each row. Today, none of the avenue's stones survive, and the ditch and embankments are severely eroded. Excavations conducted in 2008 at the end of the avenue uncovered evidence of a long-vanished stone circle, about 30 feet in diameter, consisting of about 25 monoliths now known as West Amesbury Henge. Some half mile northwest of Stonehenge, in an area referred to by archaeologists as Amesbury 50, there are the remains of the artificial hillock. It is now just a circular rise, about 65 feet in diameter and just a couple of feet high, but a land survey of 1913 records it as being very much larger. The exact size is not revealed, but it was referred to as a "hill"—Amesbury Hill—which it could no way be called today. Archaeologists reckon that it was originally over 20 feet high, but it seems to have been leveled by farmers in the mid-twentieth century to create an open field. Excavations and geophysics surveys conducted in 2010, initiated by the University of Birmingham and the Ludwig Boltzmann Institute for Archaeological Prospection and Virtual Archaeology of Vienna, revealed it to have likely been an artificial hill without internal structures like Silbury Hill and Gop Cairn.[7]

Like Avebury, Stonehenge was augmented around 2500 BCE with a further arrangement of stones within the ring. These are the stones we see today. In all, this new Stonehenge once consisted of well over 100 stones, which stood more than 20 feet high and weighed as much as 50 tons. Its outer circle was composed of 30 standing stones, each some 13 feet high, 7 feet wide, 3.5 feet thick, and weighing around 25 tons, spaced just over 3 feet apart in a 100-foot diameter ring. On top of them were placed 30 further 6-ton blocks—10 feet long, 3 feet wide, and 2.5 feet thick—called lintels, forming a continuous ring of rectangular arches 108 feet in diameter, the tops of the lintels standing well over 15 feet above the ground. This ring is known as the Sarsen

Circle, named after the sarsen stone, a type of hard sandstone from which it was made. Interestingly, despite how ancient stone circles are often depicted in the movies, Stonehenge is the only stone circle known to have had such arches. Immediately inside the Sarsen Circle was a simpler stone ring of 30 smaller stones, averaging about 6 feet high, 3.5 feet wide, and 2.5 feet thick, and weighing approximately 4 tons each. Known as the Bluestone Ring—as it was constructed from a particular type of dolerite rock commonly called "bluestone" due to its slightly bluish tinge—it was about 80 feet in diameter. Within this was created an open-oval arrangement of monoliths. Called the Bluestone Horseshoe because of its shape, it was made from about 20 bluestones, each about the same size as those forming the Bluestone Ring, and was some 35 feet across at its widest point. Between the oval and the circle of bluestones, there stood five massive arrangements of megaliths called trilithons. Each trilithon was formed from a pair of enormous upright sarsen monoliths, over 20 feet high and weighing up to 50 tons each, with a third sarsen stone, weighing about 8 tons, placed across the tops of them as a lintel to form a rectangular arch. As these trilithons were arranged in the same shape as the inner bluestones, this structure is known as the Trilithon Horseshoe, and measured about 45 feet across. Finally, close to the center of Stonehenge there lies a large rectangular stone. Weighing about 6 tons, this 6-foot-long megalith now lies flat on the ground. It has been called the Altar Stone, although the name is misleading as archaeologists believe that it originally stood upright as a single monolith. (The scale of the Stonehenge stones is even more impressive when we realize that the height of the standing stones just given is not their full size; to keep the stones erect, about a third of each monolith needed to be buried below the ground. The trilithon uprights, for instance, were well over 30 feet long.) Unlike Avebury, the original stone circle, constructed 500 years before these augmentations, no longer survives and is only discernible from the Aubrey Holes. As the estimated size and number of the first stones are approximately those of the bluestones now within the Sarsen Circle, it is generally thought that the original ring was composed of these same megaliths, which were moved to their present positions around 2500 BCE.[8]

Recent archaeological surveys have concluded that the avenues at both Avebury and Stonehenge were added around the same time as the central elaborations, sometime around 2500 BCE, although the smaller stone circles to which they led—the Sanctuary and West Amesbury Henge—are contemporary with the original monuments. It therefore appears that the original Avebury complex consisted of a 1000-foot-diameter ring of 100 monoliths standing about 30 feet apart, surrounded by a henge, with an artificial hill and smaller stone circle nearby, while the original Stonehenge complex was a 280-foot-diameter ring of 56 monoliths, standing about 15 feet apart, also surrounded by a henge, with an artificial hill and satellite circle nearby.[9] Although varying in size, number of stones, and height of the artificial hills, this same arrangement of monuments is found at other megalithic complexes throughout to British Isles. Stanton Drew megalithic complex in the county of Somerset in the west of England, for example, consisted of a 371-foot-diameter stone circle, surrounded by a 440-foot-wide henge, a now eroded artificial hill called Hauteville's Quoit that stands about a quarter of a mile to the north, and a 100-foot-diameter satellite ring called the Southwest Circle. This complex dates from around the same time as the original Stonehenge and Avebury monuments, but apart from an arrangement of monoliths and a second stone circle being erected to the northeast around 2000 BCE, there was no central augmentation or avenue added to the original complex.[10] In central England, 2 miles south of the village of Monyash in the county of Derbyshire, is Arbor Low, a henge about 290 feet in diameter, surrounding the fallen monoliths of a stone circle that originally consisted of some 50 stones between 8 and 10 feet high, with a smaller, now vanished, 80-foot-diameter stone circle to the south, later joined by an avenue of which the embankments are still visible. An artificial mound known as Gib Hill survives about 950 feet to the southwest, a mound that was later used for a Bronze Age burial. Far to the south, in the county of Dorset, a mile from the village of Wimborne St. Giles, sits another such complex. There, the ruins of a medieval church stand right in the middle of a 330-foot-diameter megalithic henge. Aptly known as Church Henge, the enclosing ditch and its outer embankment are both approximately 30 feet wide. Although now considerably eroded, they are thought to have originally been over 10 feet deep and high. The henge once encompassed a stone circle consisting of about 50 monoliths, though sadly none of the stones still survive, as they were broken up and used to build the church in the twelfth century. About 500 feet to the northwest, a satellite circle of some 20 monoliths that is about 100 feet in diameter, known as the North Circle, also existed until it too was destroyed in the twelfth century for building materials for the church. About the same distance to the west is the so-called Great Barrow, a 20-foot high, 130-foot-diameter artificial hillock converted into a burial site during the later Bronze Age. A huge, 820-foot-wide henge earthwork was constructed to the south of Church Henge about the same time as the elaborations were being made to Stonehenge, Avebury, and other megalithic complexes, around 2500 BCE, but the project seems to have been abandoned, as no stone circle was erected within it.[11]

These are just a few examples of the original megalithic complexes constructed around 3000 BCE as the Megalithic culture spread rapidly throughout the British Isles. All originally consisted of a large stone circle, a surrounding henge, a satellite circle, and a nearby artificial hill. And this is exactly what we find on the Orkney Island, at the Ring of Brodgar. As noted, this stone circle is about 340 feet in diameter and was originally composed of 60 stones, of which 27 remain, ranging in height from 7 to 15 feet. It is set within a 400-foot-diameter henge, the ditch about 10 feet deep and 30 feet wide, the outer embankment having eroded away due to its exposed setting. Some 450 feet southwest, there is the 130-foot-wide, 20-foot-high artificial hillock called Salt Knowe. But what about a satellite stone circle? There is only one other stone circle that still survives on the Orkney Islands: the Stones of Stenness. About a mile to the southeast of the Ring of Brodgar, the Stones of Stenness once consisted of 12 monoliths, each 15 feet tall, equally spaced in a circle of just over 100 feet in diameter. Both because of its proximity to the Ring of Brodgar, and the fact that it is joined to the larger ring by a narrow isthmus that divides two lochs, it seems likely that it was the satellite stone circle for the Brodgar megalithic complex. Astonishingly, the Ring of Brodgar has never been excavated, so we don't know its age for sure. Some researchers date it to around the same time as the building of the Sarsen Circle at Stonehenge, about 2500 BCE, whereas others place it around the same time as the original Stonehenge, about 3000 BCE. The Stones of Stenness *have* been excavated, however, and dated to around 3100 BCE (see chapter 6). If this was Brodgar's satellite circle, it would date the original complex to the same period.[12] This early date would make sense; as we have seen, the Megalithic culture spread south from the Orkney Islands to reach the south of England by 3000 BCE, as demonstrated by monuments such as Avebury and Stonehenge. Now we know that an almost identical complex already existed on the Orkney Islands at least a thousand years earlier.

The megalithic complex discovered on the seabed of the Bay of Firth seems to have originally consisted of a henge earthwork, 450 feet in diameter, encompassing a 350-foot-diameter stone circle of about 60 stones up to 15 feet high, with a 130-foot-wide artificial mound, some 450 feet southwest of the circle. There is also evidence of a satellite stone circle about 300 feet to the southeast, in the form of several stones, between 10 and 15 feet long, that do not seem to be natural formations.[13] This all implies that the Bay of Firth complex was copied, almost identically, on the mainland as sea levels rose, surviving as the Ring of Brodgar, Stenness, and Salt Knowe monuments. From that time, the culture spread rapidly throughout the British Isles, where similar complexes—such as Stonehenge, Avebury, Stanton Drew, and others—were created. We saw in chapter 1 that what is now the Bay of Firth began to submerge around 4000 BCE. The henge earthwork surrounding the monument may have kept the waters back for a while, but it would certainly not have stopped the encroachment of the North Sea for long. When it was abandoned, another similar complex might have been erected on land that was also later submerged (maybe to be rediscovered by future seabed surveys), and ultimately the Brodgar complex was created to replace it around 3100 BCE.

The Bay of Firth megalithic complex began sinking around 4000 BCE, so it must have been created sometime before that, perhaps around 4500 BCE when the highlands of Fairland finally submerged. If the inhabitants of Fairland did migrate to the Orkney Islands, bringing their stone-circle building culture with them, then we can surmise that they had previously constructed megalithic complexes like Brodgar, as well as the original Stonehenge, Avebury, Stanton Drew, and others, in their homeland.

So, what else do we know about the Megalithic culture of the British Isles that might have been inherited from an earlier civilization on Fairland?

About the same time as the first megalithic complexes were being created, hundreds of smaller stone circles were erected throughout the British Isles. A typical example is the Nine Ladies stone circle in the county of Derbyshire in north-central England. Standing on a hill in the Stanton Moorlands, it remains remarkably complete: nine stones about 3 feet high, in a ring just over 30 feet in diameter. There is also a single standing stone some 130 feet to the southwest in alignment with the midwinter sunset as seen from the center of the circle. (Recall that these outlying stones—the so-called king stones—are a common feature of the smaller stone circles, and some megalithic complexes were placed in the direction of either sunset or sunrise on important days of the year such as both the midwinter and midsummer solstices.) Far away, in the southwest of England near Land's End in Cornwall, stands the Merry Maidens stone circle, 19 granite megaliths, each 4 feet tall, spaced about 11 feet apart in a ring some 78 feet in diameter. Near the town of Winterbourne Abbas in the county of Dorset in southern England is the Nine Stones circle, a 30-foot ring of megaliths up to 6 feet tall, of which seven now survive. And in the north of England, on Rombald's Moor in the county of Yorkshire, are the Twelve Apostles, a stone circle that once consisted of 20 stones up to 5 feet high in a ring some 50 feet in diameter, of which only 12 remain. These are just a few examples of more than 1000 such stone circles that still survive all over the British Isles. As they were built right from the start of the Megalithic era around 3000 BCE, they may have been a feature of the Fairland landscape that the Neolithic inhabitants of the British Isles decided to adopt.

No similar, isolated, small stone circles have been identified on the Orkney Islands, but the region may not have needed them. As discussed, the megalithic complexes were created in the higher population areas, such as around Stonehenge and Avebury, while the smaller stone circles seem to have served more remote, less densely populated regions. The inhabited Orkney Islands were approximately equal to the estimated size of the tribal districts boasting megalithic complexes, so perhaps the islands' population lived close enough to the main complex to not need further, smaller circles. Large parts of the Orkney Islands have never been the focus of geophysical surveys, so alternatively it is quite possible that smaller stone circles did exist here and were at some time in the past broken up for building materials, the fate that befell so many stone circles on the mainland.[14]

In addition to the large complexes and smaller stone circles, right from the beginning of the Megalithic age the people of the British Isles erected solitary standing stones known as menhirs, coming from the old Celtic words for "long stones"—*maen* ("stone") and *hir* ("long"). These solitary monoliths stood alone and isolated from the stone circles. As archaeologists have found no evidence that they were grave markers, their purpose is a mystery. They vary from just a couple feet to over 20 feet high and, as their name implies, are generally tall and slender, the average being about 8 feet high, 3 feet wide, and 2 feet thick. They tend to taper toward the top, although that may be due to weathering. However, there are numerous examples of other, different shapes and sizes. It is impossible to know just how many once stood throughout the British Isles, but some researchers have suggested there may have been over twenty thousand. There is no official estimate of how many still exist, but it is certainly in the thousands. Like the other megalithic monuments, they survive mainly in less populated areas like the boggy uplands of Dartmoor in the county of Devon. Here, many remain, like the Beardown Man, the Loughtor Man, and the Harbourne Man, ranging between 8 and 11 feet tall, which all stand alone on the windswept moors.[15] These are examples where the word *man* has replaced the earlier word *maen* for such stones, but in nearby Cornwall, where the Celtic language was spoken longer than elsewhere in England, the old name for the isolated standing stones is still found, such as Boswen's Menhir near the town of St. Just, Trevorgan's Menhir near the village of St. Buryan, and Try Menhir near the village of Newmill.

These solitary standing stones can be found all over the British Isles and vary greatly in shape and size. In the county of Hereford in west-central England, for example, we find a variety of different shapes, typifying the diversity of such monoliths found elsewhere. We have the usual tall, slender ones, like the Pentre House Stone, which measures 10 feet tall, 3.5 feet wide, and 2.5 feet thick, now lying flat and overgrown in woodland close to the village of Bredwardine. Then there are shorter ones, such as the 4-foot-high, 1.5-foot-wide Wergins Stone near the town of Hereford, which stands in the middle of an open meadow, surrounded by a rather ugly metal framework for its protection. And there are bulky ones, like the Queen Stone in a farmer's field near the town of Goodrich—over 7 feet high and 5 feet wide, this squat megalith is heavily grooved by millennia of rainfall.[16]

Hundreds of menhirs survive in Wales too. In North Wales, near the town of Criccieth in the county of Gwynedd, is the Betws Fawr (Big Chapel) standing stone. About 8 feet tall, it stands serenely among grazing cattle in a grassy pasture. In Mid Wales, in the bleak mountains of the Brecon Beacons, stands the 12-foot-tall Maen Llia, Llia's Stone in English (it still retains its Celtic name as modern Welsh is derived directly from the ancient Celtic tongue). And in South Wales, on the edge of a scenic forest in the valley of the River Usk near the village of Llangynidr, is the aptly named Fish Stone—14 feet high and 4 feet wide at its broadest, it is shaped like an enormous fish standing upright on its tail.[17]

Because of its extensive regions of wilderness, Scotland probably has more surviving menhirs than any other part of Britain. Typical of the more accessible examples are the 9-foot-high, 4-foot-wide Airthrey Stone, which stands beside a playing field on the campus of the University of Stirling; the 10-foot-tall Macbeth's Stone in the grounds of Belmont Castle near Dundee, named after the famous eleventh-century Scottish king who is reputed to have killed a sworn enemy nearby; and an 11-foot-tall menhir that stands right beside the busy A949 road near Loch Ospisdale in the north of Scotland—called *Clach a'Charra* ("stone of vengeance" in Gaelic), it is said that enemies of the local clan were hanged on a tree that once stood beside it.[18]

Fig. 7.2. Some of the larger menhirs and standing stones in Wales and near the Welsh borders.

There were many menhirs in Ireland too, but because of its long Catholic history many of them have been re-carved and transformed into Celtic crosses.

The largest of all surviving menhirs in the British Isles stands in the graveyard of All Saints Church in the village of Rudston in the county of Yorkshire. At 25 feet high, it dwarfs the Christian tombstones around it. Many of these solitary standing stones can be found in the Orkney Islands, dating from around the same time as the Stones of Stenness. For example, on Rousay Isle stands the Yetnasteen menhir, a solitary monolith around 7 feet high, its name derived from old Norse ("Giant Stone"). There is also the 14-foot-high Sorquoy Stone near St. Margaret's Hope, and the 7-foot Setter Stone on the Isle of Eday.

So, the earliest megalithic monuments in Great Britain were complexes—consisting of a large stone circle, a henge, a satellite circle, and an artificial hill—smaller stone circles, and solitary menhirs. But what we know of them suggests that were not, like medieval churches or ancient Egyptian temples, built to a precise and strict design. Although consisting of the same cluster of monuments, the original megalithic complexes were not identical by any means. The main circles were of varying diameters, and consisted of differing numbers and sizes of stones. The same applies to the satellite circles. The artificial hillocks also varied in size, neither of these constructions seeming to have been placed in any standard direction in relation to the main ring. The smaller, isolated stone circles also differed significantly in size, while the height and number of their stones varied considerably. And the menhirs measured anything from just a couple of feet high to 25 feet high, or perhaps even bigger. The purpose of these monuments remains a mystery and is something we shall return to later. For now, it seems possible that, as this megalithic tradition began abruptly on the Orkney islands over a thousand years earlier, such monuments may have been the vestiges of a civilization that previously existed on the now-sunken isle of Fairland.

8
Megalithic Civilization
....
Orcadian Innovation

The archaeological evidence reveals that during the fourth millennium BCE, a completely new, far more advanced culture than anything that came before suddenly began on the Orkney Islands. And there is nowhere—at least, still on dry land—where it could have originated. Not in Scandinavia or mainland Europe. Even if we stretch credibility and include all of Asia, the Americas, and even the Arctic, there is nothing remotely like the Megalithic culture to be found. Its stone circles, arrangement of monuments, type of pottery, and many other features were unique to the British Isles. And it seems to have begun abruptly, fully formed with all its know-how, on the Orkney Islands around 6,000 years ago. The skills required to develop these new innovations had to have been learned by trial and error over a long period of time, yet they seem to have occurred virtually overnight, without any known precursors to the monuments and technological advances we find. The expertise had to have been developed somewhere—and it is surely beyond coincidence that this Megalithic culture appeared at exactly the time the last parts of Fairland were being submerged. It could have been from a civilization on Fairland that these technical innovations came. These abrupt changes seemed to have occurred on the Orkney Islands from as early as 4000 BCE, but were not adopted by the rest of the British Isles until around a thousand years later. We shall return to the question of why this might have been. For now, let's examine what these sudden advances were.

As well as complexes, stone circles, artificial hills, and menhirs, other new constructs abruptly appeared at the start of the Megalithic age. To begin with, the style of tombs and burials suddenly changed.

Throughout Britain, before the Megalithic culture swept rapidly south around 3000 BCE, burial monuments had been of two types—long barrows (*barrow* being an early English word for a mound) and portal tombs. (As discussed in chapter 10, these structures were built by a separate people that originated in the Iberian peninsula.)

The oldest long barrow to survive intact is thought to be the West Kennet Long Barrow, not far from Avebury in south-central England, which dates from around 3600 BCE. It is an earthen and chalk mound approximately 330 feet long and 80 feet wide, rising to a height of over 10 feet. From one end, a passage, well over 6 feet high, with two pairs of alcoves off to the sides, leads to a 10-foot-square chamber about 40 feet inside the mound. The structure, still intact after five and a half millennia, was made from large monoliths, standing upright, or laid one above the other and joined by heavy lintel stones, before being covered with earth and rubble to form the grassy mound. Outside, the single entrance is flanked by further huge stones, the largest over 12 feet tall and weighing more than 20 tons. When excavated, the barrow contained the skeletal remains of about 50 people interred over generations.[1]

Such long barrows—earthen mounds, much longer than wide, containing internal stone-lined chambers—are found throughout much of Britain. Over 150 still survive in England alone.

Another example is Wayland's Smithy near the town of Uffington in the county of Wiltshire. Dating from around 3500 BCE, it is smaller but of similar construction to the West Kennet Long Barrow: a rock-chambered tomb covered with earth, its entrance flanked by four shaped standing stones, the tallest of which is over 10 feet high. The barrow is 43 feet wide and 185 feet long, and is thought to have contained the remains of as many as fourteen bodies. (Its present name dates from the Anglo-Saxon period, over four thousand years after it was built, when legend told how it was created by Wayland the Smith, a mythical Anglo-Saxon figure who forged weapons for the gods.) There were many such long barrows, thought to have been built between around 3600 and 3000 BCE, scattered throughout southern Britain. Archaeologists have determined that the outside perimeters of such barrows were originally supported by drystone walls, but of particular interest is that for some unknown reason the burial chambers were limited to only one end of the barrow. About four times longer than wide, the mounds sloped away from the entrance to the lower end, and around two-thirds of the structure mysteriously contained no further chambers or evidence of burials or grave goods.

Long barrows seem to have been created as tombs for individuals of a special status. As they contained the remains of children as well as male and female adults, they were probably reserved for tribal leaders and their families.[2] Archaeologists have estimated that with the builders using simple Stone Age tools, construction of such long barrows as West Kennet and Wayland's Smithy would have been extensive and back-breaking endeavors but could have been accomplished within around a decade. As these tombs had movable stone "doorways," it is possible that they were also used as shrines that could be periodically opened, not only for new interments but also for ceremonies concerning ancestor worship.

In addition to the long barrows, the same period saw the creation of far more, but smaller, portal tombs. These consisted of a close arrangement of standing stones, usually three or four, which supported a large capstone to form a burial chamber. The entire structure was then covered with earth to create a mound. Today, most of these burial mounds have eroded away, leaving only the skeleton of original megaliths to appear something like a giant stone table standing alone on the landscape. These exposed structures are commonly known as *dolmens,* a name thought to originate from an old Celtic term meaning "stone table."[3]

Dolmens exist in considerable numbers throughout Britain and Ireland, and one of the largest is in south west Wales. Called the Pentre Ifan (Ivan's Village) Dolmen, it consists of an 18-ton capstone that is 16 feet long, 8 feet wide, and 3 feet thick, held 8 feet off the ground by three standing stones; three other, smaller monoliths remain, which had once flanked and sealed the entrance when the structure was covered by a mound. Another typical dolmen, a 14-ton, 18-foot-long capstone supported by three 5-foot-tall upright monoliths, is Lanyon Quoit in the county of Cornwall, in the extreme southwest of England (*quoit* is another old name for such a monument). Also, in the county of Cornwall, on Bodmin Moor, there stands Trethevy Quoit, which consists of a 12-foot long, 10-ton sloping capstone supported by five upright monoliths, the tallest standing about 9 feet high. Poulnabrone Dolmen in western Ireland has a 12-foot-long, relatively thin capstone, held 6 feet above the ground by four monoliths. Spinster's Rock in the county of Devon, in England's West Country, has a 14-foot by 10-foot 16-ton capstone, supported 8 feet above the ground by three standing stones. In the county of Oxfordshire in central England, there stand the Whispering Knights, a collapsed dolmen consisting of four uprights, the tallest about 8 feet high, with its capstone now flat on the ground. And in the extreme southeast of England, in the county of Kent, is the quaintly named Kit's Coty House, which consists of three 8-foot upright stones supporting a capstone measuring 13 by 9 feet. These are just a few of the hundreds of dolmens that still survive in the British Isles; most of them, however, only remain as fallen stones.

These dolmens date from between 3600 and 3000 BCE, the same time frame as the long barrows, so presumably they belonged to the same culture. Archaeologists believe that the mounds that covered them were built to a similar design to that of the long barrows: much longer than wide, with the burial chamber situated at one end. Essentially, they would have been less elaborate long barrows with an entrance leading directly into the chamber (rather than having a passage for access—hence the archaeological term, *portal tomb*). The reason long barrows have tended to survive as mounds, whereas portal tombs have eroded, is that the barrow mounds were built from both earth and chunks of rock. These dolmens, covered only with earth, were probably built by smaller or poorer communities, where a lack of sufficient resources or labor prohibited the creation of the more elaborate constructions. Nonetheless, both structures would have been considerable undertakings for the time. Large stones had to be quarried, shaped, and then dragged to where they were erected, and the capstones were probably hauled into place once mounds of earth were stacked around them to form ramps.[4]

Suddenly, around 3000 BCE, these tombs were abandoned, and a new type of burial structure appeared, the so-called passage tombs, so named because their burial chambers are accessed by long passageways. However, like the other features of Megalithic culture, these passage tombs appear on the Orkney Islands much earlier.

A typical passage tomb is the Quanterness Cairn on the eastern side of Mainland Island, which dates from around 3600 BCE. This circular burial mound has a diameter of about 100 feet, is 13 feet high, and is entered by a low, 30-foot-long, stone-lined passage. At the heart of the mound is a 20-foot-long, 5-foot-wide, 10-foot-high central chamber created from large, shaped stones, which the passageway enters halfway along. And from the central chamber, six short, narrow tunnels lead to side chambers, each about 6 feet long and 4 feet wide, two to each side and one at each end. It was in these side chambers that the skeletal human remains of 157 individuals were found—representatives of many generations thought to have been buried between 3600 and 3000 BCE.[5]

These new burial mounds are sometimes called Maeshowe-style tombs, named after the best-preserved example, which stands about half a mile to the east of the Stones of Stenness. As we have seen, the Maeshowe mound is 115 feet in diameter and rises to a height of 24 feet. Its low entrance passage is 3 feet high and about 36 feet long, leading to a 12-foot-high square chamber, measuring about 15 feet on each side. Some of the larger stones used to create Maeshowe weigh over 3 tons. The central chamber is constructed of flat stone slabs, many traversing the entire sides of the chamber, with the top part of the walls constructed of overlapping slabs to create a beehive-shaped roof. In each corner is a cleverly designed buttress to support the ceiling, each made from stacked stones, together with a large standing stone about 8 feet high. Three side chambers, or cells, averaging about 6 feet by 5 feet and about 3 feet high, are accessed by 2.5-foot-square entrances, each built halfway along the side and rear walls. Today, a large stone, presumably used to seal them, lies on the floor outside each of these cells.[6]

Maeshowe has been emptied by a variety of tomb robbers and souvenir hunters over the centuries, including the Vikings, who even left graffiti at the site. Nordic runes (the old Scandinavian alphabet) dating from the twelfth century are found all over the walls of the central chamber. Many tell us who carved them—such names as Vermundr, Thorir, and Haermund Hardaxe—while others include various lewd comments boasting of sexual exploits. Consequently, little in the way of human remains has survived for modern archaeologists to examine. Nonetheless, enough has been discovered in recent years, such as shards of grooved ware pottery, to date Maeshowe as being in use between around 3000 and 2600 BCE. Estimates for the time needed to build Maeshowe vary between forty thousand and one hundred thousand hours of work; either way, it required vast effort and enormous commitment. Of particular interest is that the long, straight entrance passage at Maeshowe is constructed to let the direct light of the setting sun illuminate the central

Fig. 8.1. Sometimes tombs were built adjoining megalithic stone circles, possibly for the burial of a priestly class the Romans later referred to as Druids.

chamber at the midwinter solstice around December 21. Undoubtedly, this was more than coincidence. It therefore seems likely that the Maeshowe-style mounds were more than just tombs. Some scholars propose that they were used primarily as ceremonial sites, the burials being secondary, in a similar manner to how medieval cathedrals were principally places of worship, although they also contained crypts in which the dead were laid to rest.[7]

Seven passage tombs still survive on the Orkney Islands, although there were no doubt many more that have been lost to the sea. The most spectacular is the so-called Tomb of the Otters (as otter bones were found within it), also known as the Banks Chambered Tomb, near Burwick on the island of South Ronaldsay. Here, a burial site of the same passage and chamber arrangement as other Maeshowe-style tombs is quarried out from solid rock. With about the same inner dimensions as the Quanterness Cairn, it was an astonishing feat of Neolithic

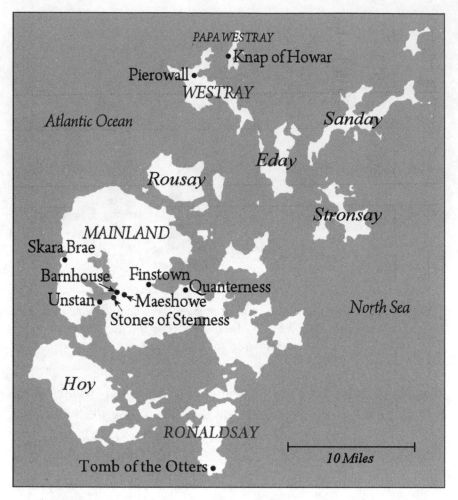

Fig. 8.2. The Orkney Islands, showing sites and locations discussed.

engineering. Only discovered in 2010, it is still being excavated, but so far thousands of human bones have been found, dated variously between 4000 and 3000 BCE, meaning that the tomb was used for the interment of successive generations for an entire millennium between 4000 and 3000 BCE.[8]

In the Irish Republic there stands the largest of all passage tombs in the British Isles. Newgrange, which lies 5 miles west of the town of Drogheda in county Meath on Ireland's eastern coast, is a mound about 250 feet across and 40 feet high, over twice the size of Maeshowe. Constructed in a similar design to Maeshowe, the mound is entered by a 60-foot-long stone passage, averaging about 5 feet in height, which leads to a rectangular chamber with a corbelled roof, measuring 21 feet long, 17 feet wide, and 20 feet high. Like Maeshowe, it has three side chambers, one to the back and one on each side of the central chamber as viewed from the end of the passage. Also, like Maeshowe, the passage is directly aligned so that the rays of the sun on the midwinter solstice shine directly into the central chamber, although at Newgrange it occurs at sunrise rather than sunset.

Various dates, ranging over a period of more than a century, have been estimated for the construction of Newgrange, with most tourist information providing a date of 3200 BCE.[9] If correct, this would mean that Megalithic culture reached here from the Orkneys around two centuries earlier than the rest of the British Isles. However, the dating should be treated with caution. The monument was in a severely dilapidated condition until it was restored in the late 1960s and early 1970s.* Examination of organic remains from the site made before this time obtained a central date of around 3200 BCE, but it was only after Newgrange was reconstructed that a more reliable form of radiocarbon dating, incorporating a process called accelerator mass

---

*During reconstruction of the tomb in the 1970s, irregular-shaped white quartz rocks, most less than a foot in size, which had previously littered the area around the front of the monument, were assembled into a 20-foot-high wall curving around the façade. The result is certainly impressive, but there is now considerable doubt among archaeologists that Newgrange originally had such a feature. It seems most unlikely that such a high, vertical wall of these stones could have been built five thousand years ago; those who created it in the 1970s needed to fix the stones in place with concrete to prevent the whole thing from collapsing. When the monument was originally built, the technology simply did not exist to fasten such a high retaining wall at such a steep angle. It is now thought that these quartz rocks were cobblestones that lined a terrace or plaza on the ground before the entrance.

spectrometry, was achieved. The problem was that the rebuilding of the tomb meant that organic remains were contaminated, making it difficult to accurately date the structure with the more precise technique. It has therefore been left to dating of pottery (p. 103) excavated at the site to determine its age, and this has resulted in a date of around 3000 BCE, approximately the same date as the original Stonehenge and other earlier megalithic monuments on the British and Irish mainland.

The building of passage tombs in mainland Britain began at the same time as the first stone circles and other megalithic monuments appeared. On the west coast of the Welsh island of Anglesey, for example, is the passage tomb of Barclodiad y Gawres. Until excavations in the 1950s it was in such a poor condition that it looked like a big pile of stones, which led to its name; in Welsh, *barclodiad y gawres* means "apronful of the giantess." Local legend tells how the mound was created when a lady giant dumped a stack of stones she had been carrying in her apron. About 90 feet in diameter, with a 20-foot entrance passage leading to a chamber with three smaller chambers to the back and sides, the tomb is basically a scaled-down version of Newgrange. Its chambers have long since collapsed, and after excavations in the 1950s a concrete roof was constructed to preserve the interior.[10] Although at Barclodiad y Gawres the entrance is aligned almost due north, meaning it was not aligned to the sun at any time of the year, at the contemporary passage tomb of Bryn Celli Ddu ("Dark Grove Mound"), on the island's southeast side, the passage is aligned to the sunrise on the summer solstice.[11]

The skills to create these kinds of structures would have taken generations to perfect. We know that such structures were first built on the Orkney Islands and later copied on the mainland British Isles, but there is no evidence of trial and error on the Orkney archipelago—such as earlier, less sophisticated structures which preceded these remarkable passage tombs. (Even the Egyptian pyramids had precursors, such as step pyramids, and early steep, straight-sided versions that invariably collapsed.) This absence of evidence of progression is also true for the other Megalithic innovations that suddenly appeared on the Orkney Islands in the early fourth millennium BCE.

The pre-Megalithic inhabitants of the British Isles, known as the Barrow culture (after their tombs), lived in temporary communities where they planted crops such as wheat and barley and raised herds of sheep, pigs, and cattle. They had not yet learned to weave, so clothing would chiefly have been garments made from animal hide. From examination of the human bones of the period, it seems that the average life span was between 30 and 35 years. Permanent settlements were rare, with these farming communities moving location every few years. The intricacies of crop cultivation had not yet been mastered, so once the nutrients of a piece of land had been depleted, the settlement would move to some other fertile location nearby. After a while the land had lain fallow for long enough to regenerate, so the community could return to a previous settlement. For this reason, buildings were made from wood, with stone structures being reserved for the dead. Long barrows and portal tombs likely served a succession of generations whose settlements were moved regularly around them; they probably served as the central point of a rotating community made up of a just a few hundred people.[12]

Then, around 3000 BCE, on the mainland British Isles the population suddenly began employing what is known as crop rotation, alternatively planting different types of crops in a system of divided fields so that the land would be replenished and remain fertile.[13] Accordingly, permanent settlements with many thousands of inhabitants quickly sprang up, such as Durrington Walls near Stonehenge, which had 1,000 dwellings and 5,000 people. The people also appear to have abruptly invented the weaving loom. Archaeological finds do not directly record evidence of weaving, as fabrics would long since have rotted away; however, their use can be discerned from the discovery of implements used in their manufacture, such as bone spindles, whorls, needles, and stone weights for twining thread. Also, remarkably, imprints of fabrics have been found on pottery, where clothing or matting pushed against the clay before it was fired. From such evidence, it is known that the Neolithic people of the period in question had woven straw mats, plant fiber carpeting and probably wall hangings, and woven and woolen blankets and clothing.[14] Various Stone Age tools discovered at Neolithic settlements of the time also tell that they made baskets, ropes, and nets. Additionally, around 3000 BCE, the early Megalithic people of the British Isles suddenly began using a new, more sophisticated style of pottery. Known as grooved ware, it gets its name from the characteristic grooved designs that decorated the rims of the unusual (for the time), flat-bottomed, straight-sided pots (which took considerable skill to make), the remains of which have been found all over the British Isles.[15] For some years, scientists have been able to date ceramic material using thermoluminescence and rehydroxylation (p. 103)[16] and by using a combination of these techniques, archaeologists have been able to determine the progressive use of grooved ware pottery as it moved south over just a few decades around 3000 BCE, beginning in the north of Scotland. Earlier pottery in the British Isles consisted of round-bottomed bowls; the more practical, harder-wearing, flat-bottomed grooved ware was something of a leap in ceramic making, requiring better stone kilns and firing techniques.[17]

All these dramatic developments—crop rotation, the weaving loom, and ceramic manufacture—had originated on the Orkney Islands up to a thousand years earlier than elsewhere in the British Isles, before spreading south around 3000 BCE. The Orcadians (inhabitants of the Orkney Islands) should have taken years of trial and error to perfect these innovations, yet these advances seem to have just sprung into existence in no time at all. These developments, along with the megalithic monuments and distinctive passage tombs we have examined, all far more elaborate than anything that came before, were the distinctive features of Megalithic culture that spread though the British Isles around 5,000 years ago. And it all began suddenly on the Orkney Islands. Before 4000 BCE, when these innovations first appeared as if from nowhere, the inhabitants of the Orkney Island were less advanced than their southern neighbors. They hadn't gotten around to building anything like the contemporary long barrows or portal tombs constructed in the rest of the British Isles. Far from it, the Orkney dwellers seem to have existed as simple, extended family communities along the coastline, living mainly on seaweed, fish, and other sea creatures, venturing inland to hunt and gather. (They had simple boats that could carry at most two people, constructed of hide stretched around a modest wicker frame.) Clothes were made primarily from seal and walrus hide, pottery was simple and fired in open-pit kilns, and utensils were far less sophisticated than those on the mainland.[18]

But then everything abruptly changed: the characteristic megalithic monuments began to be erected, and the technical innovations in pottery, weaving, and farming suddenly appeared. The Orcadians even began building stone houses—the first anywhere in Europe. A Neolithic farmstead called the Knap of Howar on the island of Papa Westray consists of two adjacent thick-walled buildings with low doorways. The larger structure, which may have served as a workshop, is linked to the other building by a low passageway. The interior of the dwelling house is partitioned by further walls, and the house contains fireplaces as well as low stone frameworks into which dried seaweed and bracken are thought to have been placed to form beds. Even stone storage shelves still survive intact, while postholes indicate that there was once a roof structure, probably made from thatched straw waterproofed with seal fat. These remarkably well-preserved buildings were originally thought to be an astonishing 5,700 years old, but the latest estimates, made possible by the rehydroxylation dating of pottery fragments found beneath the walls, have pushed back the time of construction even further, to around 4000 BCE. Radiocarbon dating of animal bones discarded around the site suggests the place was occupied for about a thousand years until around 3000 BCE. The Knap of Howar is the best-preserved such site, but archaeologists have discovered clusters dotted all around the Orkney Islands of other, similar, less-well preserved buildings thought to date from the fourth millennium BCE.[19]

These isolated farmsteads once stood some distance from the shore (before land was lost to the sea), whereas it is believed that most settlements, as fishing communities, would have been built much closer to the sea. As such, the rise in sea level between 4000 and 3000 BCE would have pushed the shoreline ever farther inland, submerging many of them. One, though, miraculously survived. It is reckoned to be one of the last such settlements to have been created around 3100 BCE, as the encroaching waters began to relent. Called Skara Brae, this Neolithic village stands on the coast, some 6 miles northwest of the Stones of Stenness and the Ring of Brodgar, which were erected around the same time. It was probably the home of some of the very people who not only used the megalithic complex but also built it. This ancient settlement has been uncovered by archaeologists and found to have consisted of a group of clustered stone-wall dwellings. Set into the ground with only their thatch-covered roofs once visible above the surface, the layout of this astonishing underground settlement, with its houses connected by a series of tunnels, was a clever way to keep warm and dry in the cold, damp climate of the windswept Orkney Islands. This—the best-preserved Neolithic village anywhere in the world—consisted of seven clustered dwellings composed of single, rounded rooms each measuring an average of 400 square feet. Each room was entered through a low doorway sealed with a stone slab that could be slid open and shut. Remarkably, the homes still contained pieces of furniture, such as closets, shelving, seats, and storage boxes, and hearth areas, all made from stone. Even beds still survived, consisting of a rectangle of stone slabs, probably once filled with straw overlaid by animal hides. An eighth building has no such furnishings, but was divided into cubicles, and seems to have been used as a workplace for making tools such as bone needles, stone axes, and flint knives. Amazingly, a drainage system, consisting of stone channels, was incorporated into the overall design of the settlement, including a toilet in each house in the form of a stone-divided cubicle.[20] It may not seem like much by today's standards, but compared with anything else in the British Isles at the time, this was the height of luxury. When Skara Brae was being established, the inhabitants of the rest of the British Isles had yet to create permanent, stone-built settlements; elsewhere dwellings were made primarily from wood, brush, and mud.[21]

There were other contemporary villages like Skara Brae on the islands, up to twice the size, but none have remained anywhere near as well preserved. One such village is just to the north of the Stones of Stenness, on the shores of the Loch of Harry. Called the Barnhouse Settlement, it was excavated in the 1980s to reveal that it originally consisted of about fifteen dwellings like those at Skara Brae. There were probably dozens of such ancient Neolithic villages dotted around the Orkney Islands, some home to well over a hundred people. The fragmentary remains of some of these settlements have been identified, but it is thought that, as most were built close to shore, many have been lost to the ocean due to rising sea levels and the erosion of the exposed coastline.[22] Some, buried beneath the ground, may still await discovery. Today around twenty thousand people inhabit the islands, which is approximately the same number of people who lived there when records began in 1801. While it is impossible to tell just how many people lived on the Orkneys between five and six thousand years ago, it must have been a thriving population.

Leaving aside how the Megalithic culture got started, and whether it originated on Fairland, there is a further mystery: Why did it remain isolated on the Orkney Islands for a thousand years before spreading south onto the mainland British Isles? We can only assume that being 20 miles north of the mainland British Isles, where the people were still living mainly as Barrow-culture travelers (p. 133) and many were still little more than hunter-gatherers, the Orcadians saw no reason to migrate. They had everything they needed right where they were. It's what made them change their mind that's the mystery.

You have probably noted how we repeatedly learn of monuments and dwellings on the Orkney Islands being abandoned around 3000 BCE. After centuries of occupation or use, places like the Knap of Howar, Quanterness Cairn, and the Tomb of the Otters were completely abandoned. There was clearly some kind of depopulation around this time, and it wasn't due to rising sea levels. By 3000 BCE the waters had ceased rising. Interestingly, though, it wasn't a complete evacuation of the islands. Skara Brae, for instance, continued to be occupied until it was completely covered by sand during a freak storm around 2500 BCE (which is why it is so well preserved).[23] Pottery at Maeshowe and evidence of human activity, such as feasting, found at the Brodgar complex show that both monuments continued to be used for some centuries after 3000 BCE.

Archaeologists believe that the most likely explanation for a partial exodus from the Orkney Islands around 5,000 years ago is that the islands had become deforested. Evidence from soil core samples taken throughout the archipelago has revealed that the Orkneys were once covered by thick-forested areas, with open woodland and arable farmland on the hillsides. Over the years the inhabitants used more and more wood, until ultimately it was all gone, and the Orkneys became what they remain today—virtually treeless, windswept heathland.[24] The lack of trees meant that fertile soil could easily be eroded, and farming all but ceased. The Orcadians could still make a living from the sea, so there was no reason for the entire population to leave. But many of them clearly did to make their way to the Scottish mainland in the hope of starting a new life. From around 4000 BCE, the islanders had started building far more sophisticated boats than they had before. Large, hide-covered canoes with stabilizing outriggers—similar to traditional Hawaiian canoes—were capable of carrying more than a dozen people, as well as caged animals and supplies, to the mainland in fair weather.[25] The Orcadians took with them their culture and expertise, which was rapidly adopted by tribe after tribe throughout the British Isles. This, then, is probably how the Megalithic culture came to the British Isles. Before assessing in detail how the Orcadian culture originally began, and examining crucial evidence concerning a preceding civilization on Fairland, we need to consider Megalithic thinking. In short, why did they build their enigmatic monuments?

9

Geomancers and Healers

....

Purpose of the Monuments

Numerous archaeological digs and geophysics surveys have uncovered absolutely no evidence that menhirs were ever used as grave markers. They may have been erected to honor ancestors, venerate gods, or perhaps, as some researchers have suggested, to act as giant sundials. Intriguingly, however, these solitary monoliths may not have been so solitary at all, but part of a much larger pattern of megalithic stones.

There are many examples of menhirs having been erected in what were clearly intended to be alignments. For example, five monoliths, each up to 22 feet high, stood in a straight line about 200 feet apart, crossing fields in the district of Boroughbridge, in northern England. Called the Devil's Arrows, only three now survive, the others having been pulled down to be used in the construction of a nearby bridge in the eighteenth century. If we take a line through this alignment and continue in a northwest direction for 5 miles, it passes through the Cana Barn and Hutton Moor henge circles. Furthermore, geophysics surveys have revealed that at least three other menhirs stood directly along this alignment between the Devil's Arrows and these two henges. Another example is found at the other end of the country, in Cornwall. Here we find that a line drawn from the center of the Merry Maidens stone circle near the village of St. Buryan passes through two aligned menhirs called the Pipers to the northeast, then runs through three other standing stones before reaching the sea at Merthen Point, about one and a half miles away. Here, geophysics has revealed that a further 80-foot diameter stone circle once stood.

These are just two examples of deliberate alignments of menhirs, averaging about 100 feet apart, joining megalithic stone circles separated by some distance. There are also many examples of straight rows of megaliths where the stones are placed closer together. On Dartmoor in Devon, for instance, there are dozens of such alignments, the longest being a line of more than 800 monoliths, up to 8 feet tall and about 6.5 feet apart, stretching over a mile between the Dancers Stone Circle on Bledge Hill and a Neolithic artificial mound at Green Hill to the north. Other examples include an alignment in South Wales consisting of eight menhirs up to 9 feet tall (two are fallen and two have been removed since the nineteenth century), which runs for 120 feet near the village of Llanychaer, as well as the Madacombe stone row on Exmoor in Somerset, now consisting of 12 standing stones, which archaeologists have determined was originally made up of an alignment of many more, almost 1,000 feet long.

In 1921 the English amateur archaeologist Alfred Watkins proposed that menhirs had been raised at locations that formed straight lines, linking stone circles in a vast network covering much of the British Isles. In his book *The Old Straight Track,* published in 1925, he advocated that these menhirs were erected as markers set along age-old trackways. In addition to the obvious standing stone alignments that existed over relatively short distances, like those mentioned above, Watkins also believed that such monoliths set farther apart linked stone circles, Neolithic settlements, and various megalithic monuments over much greater distances. They either acted as marker stones, he argued, or were sacred pillars located along the ancient roads that the Neolithic people once traveled, akin to the way that shrines to saints are found along modern roads in Catholic countries like Ireland. Watkins found that many of his supposed menhir alignments ran through places containing the syllable "ley" in their names, such as the villages Amberley, Bowley, and Foxley in his native county of Herefordshire in west-central England. This led him to conclude that this may have been the original word for the ancient trackways. Accordingly, he called his alignments *leys* (pronounced "lays"), and the name stuck. Today, the term *ley lines* is more familiar. The academic community was not convinced, asserting that the suggested alignments were down to pure chance.[1]

Although archaeologists were loath to accept Watkins's ideas, the hippie movement in the 1960s came to embrace them with a passion. The notion that ley lines had been processional ways or trading routes was abandoned, and instead they were seen as channels of mystical power. The first person to write about the new theory, and possibly the one who initiated it, was British author John Michell. In his book *The View Over Atlantis,* published in 1969, Michell advocated that ley lines marked conduits of "spiritual force" that ran through the earth and were tapped by ancient priests, similar to the concept of feng shui in China, and also known as geomancy. According to this hypothesis, ley lines were—or were thought by their creators to be—the ancient equivalent of electric power lines, conducting some unspecified kind of energy through the earth. These lines were sensed by Neolithic dowsers, it was proposed, and the menhirs were erected to mark their course, with stone circles being built where ley lines crossed, marking locations where the power was at its strongest.[2]

Today, New Agers still congregate at stone circles and solitary menhirs in the belief that they can, even now, experience or manipulate this magical power. The notion of ley lines as a paranormal power grid has found popularity around the globe, with many people believing that they exist throughout the world. According to this modern rendering of the theory, originally propounded to account for the apparent alignment of

British menhirs, ancient cultures all over the Earth built sacred monuments on ley lines. For the academic community, this is certainly taking things too far. Be that as it may, and returning to the Megalithic British Isles, it is certain that deliberate alignments of menhirs did exist over distances of up to 5 miles, and perhaps more. They were clearly intended to link nearby stone circles for some reason—perhaps to mark processional ways, or even to plot out what were thought to have been conduits of spiritual energy, as was done in ancient China[3] and seemingly by the people who created the Nazca Lines in southern Peru.[4] But did these menhir alignments exist over much greater distances, as Watkins believed?

The problem is that over millennia the landscape has changed unrecognizably. Farming, roads, towns, villages, cities, and all manner of infrastructure have obliterated all trace of most original standing stones. Consequently, since Watkins's time, it is not only monuments from the Megalithic era that have been used to plot ley lines. From the 1960s, all sorts of ancient sites that had nothing to do with the Neolithic period have been included: old churches, Iron Age hillforts, medieval moats, holy wells, natural springs, even castles and ruins of any kind, to name just a few. Although most of these features have no link to Neolithic times, many old churches do. They were often built over or in place of megaliths, sometimes right in the middle of stone circles. Although the Megalithic era had ended centuries before, when Christianity first became established in Britain, during both the late Roman era and post-Roman period (between the fifth and seventh centuries), many megalithic monuments were still revered by the native Britons. The early Catholic Church tended to build their places of worship on ground already considered sacred by a local population, sometimes without destroying preexisting shrines, and in the British Isles these sites included stone circles and standing stones.[5]

There are over 8,000 medieval parish churches in England alone, many having been built on the site of much earlier Roman and post-Roman chapels; a good number of these were erected within mega-lithic rings or beside standing stones. Most of these stones have long since been removed, but miraculously some have survived. As we have already seen, at Church Henge in southern England a medieval church stands inside what was a 330-foot-diameter stone circle. A Welsh example is found in the tiny hamlet of Ysbyty Cynfyn ("King Cynfyn's Hospice") in the county of Ceredigion. Here, the church of Saint John the Baptist stands in the middle of a stone circle whose megaliths, up to 11 feet high, survive in its surrounding wall. And in Scotland a remark-ably well-preserved stone circle survives in the graveyard surrounding the church at Midmar in the county of Aberdeen. It consists of seven upright monoliths, the tallest over 8 feet high, and a huge, 14-foot-long horizontal megalith weighing an estimated 20 tons, all in a circle about 55 feet in diameter. Likewise, there are numerous examples of single menhirs still seen in church graveyards. In the extreme southwest of the British Isles, for instance, there is one in the graveyard of Saint Laudus Church in the village of Mabe in Cornwall, and in the far north there is one in Strathblane churchyard in Scotland. Most are no larger than 8 feet tall, but some are much bigger: the largest of all surviving men-hirs in the British Isles is the 25-foot-high standing stone in the grave-yard of All Saints Church in Rudston.

If, when plotting potential alignments of megalithic monuments, we include medieval churches thought to have been built on the site of earlier Roman or post-Roman chapels, then we find that these features, along with standing stones, do appear to align over long distances, far more than should be expected by chance alone. Of course, the debate over ley lines rages. However, if for the sake of argument we accept that longer alignments of menhirs were indeed deliberate, then what might have been their purpose?

One interesting hypothesis was first propounded by author Tom Graves in his book *Needles of Stone,* which was published in 1978. He proposed that standing stones could tap into some manner of natural earth energy (presumably the same geomantic force advocated by John Michell) in the way that acupuncture needles allegedly manipulate the so-called meridian channels of the human body. The ancients had used the energy of ley lines, he argued, to fertilize the land, gain spiritual enlightenment, commune with deities, and induce heightened states of mind.[6] It is quite possible that this, or something like it, was indeed the belief held by the Megalithic culture. After all, similar beliefs, in the form of acupuncture and feng shui, have existed for centuries in China. Whatever the reason behind the local menhir alignments, and maybe the hypothesized leys, it's possible that, in addition to the other megalithic monuments we have examined, such stone configurations also once existed on Fairland long before being adopted by the people of the British Isles.

We turn now to the stone circles themselves. Many researchers have advocated that the megaliths of stone circles—not only the king stones (p. 97)—were deliberately placed to align with the rising and setting of the sun, moon, and particularly bright stars at specific times of the year. Keep in mind that in the distant past stars would appear to be in slightly different locations relative to Earth compared with where they are today.[7] Although stars, as opposed to the bodies of the solar system, remain in a set position compared with one another, over the course of many centuries this stellar background appears to move very slowly. Due to something called axial precession—a gradual shift in the Earth's axis of rotation, or a slow wobble—the North and South Poles appear to move in circles against the fixed backdrop of stars, taking approximately 26,000 years to complete each circuit. Accordingly, where each star rises or sets today is somewhat different from the past. The celestial alignments being proposed by researchers were determined on this basis—where the stars *had* been when the stones were erected. When first proposed in the 1960s, such theories involved complex mathematical calculations. These days, with the use of computer programs, we can determine where the stars were, as seen from Earth, at any period of history, and in the face of such modern technology the celestial alignment hypothesis does hang together. Some celestial alignments still exist today, particularly solar alignments, and may be explained by stones having been moved in the past to compensate for axial precession.[8] The average stone circle had a diameter of about 45 feet, and would originally have been composed of between 12 and 20 stones, often with a further single monolith, the king stone, standing outside the main circle and aligned to the midsummer or midwinter sunrise or sunset as seen from the center of the ring. The much larger stone circles of megalithic complexes also had king stones, such as the Heel Stone at Stonehenge, over which the sun rises on the summer solstice. The height and shape of stone circle monoliths varied, most being between 3 and 6 feet high (though some were as tall as 15 feet). These stone circles may have been of different diameters and made up of varying sizes and number of stones—thought to reflect the extent of the regional population and the workability of local rock—but celestial alignment theorists propose that they were all built around the same basic principle: a circle of standing stones with monoliths aligned to various heavenly bodies as seen from the center of the ring.

The celestial alignment theory is supported by the locations where the stone circles were built—at sites where the heavens could best be viewed. One of the many riddles concerning stone circles is that nearly all of them were constructed some distance from the communities where their creators lived. A culture's monuments or places of worship are usually built at the heart of the civilization's settlements: shrines in villages, temples in towns, and more elaborate sanctuaries in cities. During the long Megalithic era, apart from the foundations of small clusters of huts where it is thought the priesthood or custodians of the monuments may have dwelled, the nearest settlements were often miles from the stone circles. Settlements were usually sited in fertile valleys, offering such amenities as natural shelter, waterways, and good farming land, whereas the stone circles were invariably situated in locations such as open plains, barren moorlands, and exposed hills. These were settings that provided a panoramic view of the sky, which would plausibly explain why the circles were erected there: so that the firmament could be observed.

It is generally agreed that such celestial alignments indicate that megalithic stone circles were used as astronomical calculators. From the perspective of someone on Earth, the night stars move across the firmament, gradually progressing across the sky as the year goes by. A person standing in the center of a stone circle could use the monoliths to determine the exact position of a star on any day of the year, at any time of night, by where it was in relation to the stones. In other words, it would enable a seasoned observer to determine not just the date, but the precise moment of a specific day. (Such precise timepieces would not be available again until the invention of the mechanical clock.) It is thought that these stone calendars enabled the Neolithic people to determine the right time to plant, nurture, and harvest crops, as well as perhaps when to time annual ceremonial activities.[9] (A ring of wooden posts could serve the same purpose, and archaeologists have found indications of such structures, but they would be prone to movement due to weather, not to mention rot.) The mystery is that to determine the right times of the year for general horticultural purposes, such as planting and reaping, or the days of ceremonial events, you would not need such an accurate calendar. Approximate dates could be determined by the progression of the sun alone. So why the precision? It might be explained if they concerned a very special kind of horticulture.

Before speculating as to what this might have been, we need to examine a specific type of megalithic burial place that seems to have been reserved for an elite group of people. Known as "box tombs," they consisted of a rectangular structure, averaged about 12 feet long and 4 to 6 feet wide, were made up of large slabs of rock, were about 5 feet high and 6 inches thick, and were divided into two parts by a further vertical slab set widthwise across the middle. The body was buried in one section of the chamber, and grave goods were deposited in the other; a series of capstones were then placed over the top, and the entire structure was covered with a circular mound or a pile of stones. They were very different from the other burial sites used by the Megalithic people and from those of the new migrants (such as Beaker and Wessex cultures). Unlike these other tombs, they were erected beside stone circles. Here are a few examples of such box tombs found all over the British Isles:

Teergonean Tomb near the village of Doolin in County Clare, Ireland[10]

Haco's Tomb, erroneously named after a much later Viking king, near the town of Largs in North Ayrshire, Scotland[11]

Bant's Carn on the island of St. Mary's off the coast of Cornwall[12]

the Curbar Mound tomb in the hilly Peak District of Derbyshire[13]

Penywyrlod Cairn, near the village of Llanigon in the county of Powys in Wales[14]

These are just a few examples of box tombs built right next to what were, or still are, stone circles. Some stone circles even have box tombs built within them, such as:

Yellowmead stone circle near Sheepstor in Devon[15]

Fingal's Cauldron on the Isle of Arran in Scotland[16]

Castlerigg stone circle in Cumbria[17]

Callanish stone circle on the Isle of Lewis[18]

Fig. 9.1. Great Britain, showing sites discussed in this chapter.

Even the oldest stone circle to still survive on dry land—the Stones of Stenness on the Orkney Islands—once had a box tomb within it, but it was destroyed in 1814. One Captain Mackay, who leased the land on which the stones stood, deliberately attempted to remove the entire monument. Apparently, he had been angered by local people who were performing "rituals" there. Outraged, the islanders managed to put a stop to the demolition before the Stones of Stenness were destroyed, but sadly not before the box tomb was demolished. All that now survives are two of its stones, known as the cove, which were reerected inside the ring in 1907.

One particularly good example of a box tomb, where the mound has eroded and the capstones have been removed to reveal the interior structure, is the Bridestones, near Biddulph in north-central England. What had been the heart of the tomb survives as an arrangement of megalithic stones averaging about 1 foot wide and 5 feet high, creating a chamber with inner dimensions of about 6 by 14 feet, divided into two equal parts by a further, broken slab. For years the monument had been mistaken for a pre-Megalithic long barrow, due to two 10-foot mono-liths that now stand at one end, like the portal stones at monuments such as Wayland's Smithy (p. 124). However, these two stones originally lay fallen nearby, until the 1930s when members of the Department of Geography at Manchester University reerected the monoliths in their present positions, wrongly assuming they were restoring the site to its original condition.[19] Luckily, a survey of the Bridestones was made by the Welsh antiquarian Henry Rowlands in the early eighteenth century and published in his work *Mona Antiqua Restaurata* (Ancient Anglesey Restored) of 1723, which reveals how the original monument appeared. The two monoliths were originally part of a stone circle that stood right next to the tomb, all but them having been removed in the nineteenth century to be used in the construction of an ornamental garden in the area. The circle consisted of ten approximately 10-foot-tall stones in a ring about 27 feet in diameter. In Rowland's day, the box tomb still had a roof made from horizontal stone slabs and was covered by a large mound of rocks, which had fallen away at one end, exposing the chamber, and giving it the appearance of an "artificial cave."[20] (These rocks were removed in the mid-eighteenth century to be used in the construction of a nearby road.)

These box tombs were divided into two equal-sized chambers, the one side holding the body or sometimes cremated remains, the other containing precious possessions, such as jewelry and amulets. Intriguingly, when such a tomb has been in a suitable condition to be properly excavated and its finds scientifically examined, these grave goods have been found to mostly consist of ceramic jars and pots containing the long-dried extracts from plants likely to have been used for pharmaceutical purposes, such as for their analgesic, antiseptic, and curative properties. Below are just a few examples.

> Dried oil from the *Chelidonium majus,* commonly known as greater celandine, and amentoflavone obtained from juniper plants have been extracted from vessels found in a 5,000-year-old box tomb close to Maeshowe on the Orkney Islands.[21] A mixture made from the root of the former is an effective gargle for toothache and sore throats, and the latter is known for its disinfectant properties and is widely used as an ingredient in modern antiseptic creams.

> At Ashgrove in the district of Fife, Scotland, a box tomb dating from around 2500 BCE held a pottery vessel containing a substance from the flowers of the *Tilia cordata,* the small-leaved lime or linden tree, used as an infusion to treat high temperatures and break fevers (somewhat like modern acetaminophen), while another similar tomb nearby contained ceramic fragments coated with a residue made from the leaves of the *Tanacetum vulgare,* or

common tansy plant, used to treat intestinal parasites and sometimes used in modern deworming veterinary products.[22]

A cup found in a box tomb at Undy in the county of Aberdeen,
dating from around 2200 BCE, contained the residue of salicylic
acid from the buds of the *Filipendula ulmaria,* the meadowsweet
herb, an analgesic, which in the nineteenth century was used to
produce the first aspirin.[23]

An urn discovered during excavations at a box tomb at Fernworthy
on Dartmoor in Devonshire, dating from around 1500 BCE,
held the remains of the seeds of the *Datura stramonium* fruit,
also known as the thorn apple. Due to today's cooler climate, it
no longer grows naturally in the British Isles. The thorn apple
is highly toxic and produces delirium, rapid heartbeat, coma,
and death, but if properly prepared, it can result in temporary
unconsciousness when ingested.[24] Certain Native American
tribes, in areas where the plant still grows, used it to anesthe-
tize those requiring painful procedures such as amputations, and
some archaeologists have suggested that this was what the thorn
apple was used for by the ancient people of the British Isles.
Astonishingly, no effective anesthetic was rediscovered in Europe
until the synthesis of ether in the nineteenth century.

Pottery excavated in 1921 from the Penywyrlod Cairn in Wales,
dating from around 600 BCE, remained in the vaults of the
British Museum for decades before being subjected to scientific testing. The results showed that the ceramic fragments
contained the residue of a liquid made from stems of the
Scrophularia nodosa, or figwort herb, used as an effective rem-
edy for treating cuts, sores, and abrasions. Even today, extracts
from the plant are used in ointments for the relief of eczema,
psoriasis, and hemorrhoids.[25]

Box tombs nearly always contain plants that are toxic, foul tasting, or virtually inedible under normal circumstances. You certainly wouldn't eat them for nutritional purposes or as part of your diet. Most of them even lack narcotic effects that might have led to their use as recreational drugs or to induce visions.[26] Their only conceivable uses, it seems, would have been medicinal. And the box tombs that uniquely contained such materials appear to have been those used exclusively for the interment of an elite group of people associated with the stone circles where they were buried. During the period these tombs were built, the general population of the British Isles was being interred in other ways, such as in unmarked graves or simple stone cists, being laid to rest with a single beaker, or having their cremated remains deposited in urns. None of these burials included the kinds of medicinal plant extracts found in box tombs. It would therefore seem that these substances were used to make cures by the high-status individuals buried in these tombs.[27]

If the kind of noxious substances found in their graves were, as seems likely, administered as remedies to be ingested or applied to wounds or abrasions, those who prepared them must have been highly skilled herbalists—otherwise, they would have been little more than poisoners. Many of the plant extracts found in these box tombs are toxic, and for them to perform their curative functions they needed to be prepared according to precise and careful formulas. Not only would such plants require being planted and tended at a particular time of the year, but specific parts of plants—such as the seeds, roots, leaves, stems, flowers, or buds—would sometimes need to be harvested on a very specific day, and at an exact time. The chemical continuants of live vegetation alter consistently depending on their annual cycle. But plants, or the parts of plants that are highly toxic—often those used for medicinal purposes—become less poisonous at night, but only on particular days of the year. The reason for this is that the organism has evolved to deter some creatures and attract others when it is ready to be pollenated. Plants that evolved to attract night-pollinating insects change their chemical makeup during the hours of darkness in order to attract creatures like moths. Many of the substances utilized in the making of remedial potions need to be extracted at a very specific time. Even the kinds of botanical medicines that can be harvested during the hours of daylight often need to be gathered on very particular days. Creating these herbal remedies would have been an extremely complex and exact procedure.[28]

Consider the substances found in the tombs listed above. Figwort stems and leaves, for instance, need to be harvested on specific days in July and dried for later use in liquid extracts, tinctures, and ointments. If picked at the wrong time or not desiccated properly, they are useless as an irritant relief; on the contrary, their application results in painful inflammation. Unless the thorn apple is from an older bush and picked within just a few days each year, it can prove fatal, or at the very least induce severe vomiting, convulsions, and delirium. Tansy flowers bloom in July and August, but unless they are cut about halfway through this period, not only would any intestinal parasites be killed but the human host as well. Removing the salicylic acid from the meadowsweet herb for its analgesic properties is an intricate process involving the draining of sap from the herb. This must be conducted not only at specific times of the year but also at a particular time of night due to chemical changes designed to attract a particular species of moth. Extract from the root of the greater celandine is extremely poisonous, even in moderation, unless obtained at a specific time of the winter, when the perennial plant is dormant and just before it begins to return to life.[29] If you gargled with an infusion made from the stuff picked even a day or two away from the correct time, it would be like rinsing your mouth with cyanide.

These precise harvesting times might explain why stone circles were built. The position of the sun—behind, above, or between the monoliths of stone circles—could be used to determine a specific day, or time of day, whereas the positions of the stars in relation to the stones could determine an exact time of night of a particular day. (Of course, all this would depend on good weather. From the remains of vegetation excavated from archaeological sites, it is known that the British Isles during the Megalithic age were far sunnier than today.) The cultivation and harvesting of vegetation for medicinal purposes, as well as the preparation of medications, needed precise timing— something that stone circles, as precise astronomical calculators, made possible. In conclusion, the trial and error necessary to identify, grow, harvest, and prepare very specific parts of often poisonous plants, and to get their mixtures and measures just right to make viable medicines, and to perfect the megalithic astronomical calendars essential for such preparation, must have taken centuries to achieve. Yet these pharmaceutical substances appeared suddenly, with no evidence of their gradual development, on the Orkney Islands around 4000 BCE. Just like the advanced building techniques, farming practices, textile making, and ceramic manufacture that abruptly began at the start of the Megalithic age, this astonishingly advanced medicinal knowledge might also have originated on Fairland.

We turn, therefore, to this ancient land itself. Apart from a remarkably sophisticated culture that suddenly arrived on the Orkney Islands during the fourth millennium BCE, and later spread throughout the British Isles, is there any *direct* evidence that a civilization really did exist on Fairland before it sank beneath the waves?

10

Fairland

·······································

Evidence of Civilization and Migration

Landscape mapping of the bed of the North Sea (bathymetric analysis), combined with what is known about the postglacial rise in sea levels countered by isostatic adjustment (land rise), has revealed that around 7000 BCE Fairland extended some 50 miles north and 40 miles east of the present-day Orkney Islands. Its southernmost point was approximately 60 miles due east of the northern tip of Scotland, while the northernmost point was approximately 25 miles southwest of the Shetland Islands, making it around 90 miles long. At its broadest point, it was about 50 miles wide. In all, it was considerably larger than modern-day Rhode Island (48 miles long and 37 miles wide). Local isometric adjustment allowed the extent of the island to remain pretty much the same until around 5000 BCE.[1]

To recap: During the last Ice Age, compacted ice sheets more than two miles thick covered northern Britain, and their massive weight, pushing down over a period of 100,000 years, crushed the land beneath, depressing it by hundreds of feet. Once the ice retreated, the northern British Isles slowly began to rise, countering the effect of rising sea levels.[2] After 5000 BCE, as regional land rise slowed and waters continued to rise, the sea gradually began to envelop Fairland until 4000 BCE, when all but the highest land was submerged. However, most of the higher-elevation Orkney Islands to the south, as well as the Shetland Isles to the north, remained above sea level. As we have seen, a civilization that once existed on Fairland might well have initiated the Megalithic culture of the Orkney Islands sometime before 4000 BCE; the same, however, did not occur on the more remote Shetland Isles.

Archaeology on the Shetland Isles—for example, at West Voe and at Walls on Mainland Isle—have shown that until well after 3000 BCE the islands were still very much in the Mesolithic, hunter-gatherer age. (Somewhat confusingly, like the Orkneys, the Shetland's largest island is also called Mainland.) The oldest Neolithic, permanent farming communities were only established after 2500 BCE, such as the Scord of Brouster and Jarlshof in west and south Mainland. There are some impressive prehistoric monuments on the Shetlands, such as the so-called Stanydale Temple in western Mainland—the foundations of a 40-foot-diameter, circular building thought to have been a public meeting place—and the Broch of Mousa, a remarkably well-preserved round stone tower on the island of Mousa. However, these only date from the late first millennium BCE.[3] There is no evidence of any megalithic stone circles having been erected in the Shetland Islands; one monument referred to as the Hjaltadans Stone Circle, on the island of Fetlar, is in fact nothing like the kind of stone circles we find elsewhere in the British Isles. Rather, it is a 37-foot-diameter ring of 38 nearly touching, flat stones, delineating what was probably some kind of sacred enclosure. There are a few solitary standing stones, such as Bordastubble Stone and the Clivocast Stone at Unst on Shetland's most northerly island.[4] However, standing stones like these can be found in many parts of Neolithic Europe, where any evidence of true stone circles and megalithic complexes is completely absent. (For instance, the contemporary people of Brittany in northwestern France also erected standing stones, but this culture was completely different and totally separate from the Megalithic culture of the British

Isles. The Bretons built no stone circles or megalithic complexes any-thing like those found across the English Channel.) Confusingly, such monuments are sometimes described by the word *megalithic,* but this is only in the general meaning of the Greek term for "large stone," and in no way relates to the Megalithic culture of the British Isles. Shaping and raising single stones for various reasons is not unique to Megalithic culture; their location with respect to the wider array of monuments in which they are found makes them unique. Neither are there any telltale megalithic passage or box tombs on the Shetlands that date from the period when such funerary structures appear throughout the Orkneys and then the rest of the British Isles. Rather, what are known as heel cairns are unique to the Shetlands. A heel cairn is a simple, single stone chamber, accessed by a short passage-way, and covered with a shoe-heel-shaped mound, the best-preserved example being a 30-foot-diameter, 5-foot-high mound on the island of Vementry.[5] It doesn't even seem that Megalithic grooved ware pottery was adopted on the Shetlands. There is only one isolated example, known as the Sumburgh sherd, but this was probably imported and, even then, not until around 800 BCE.[6]

The Shetlanders were still practicing a Mesolithic way of life for centuries after the Orcadians had adopted the Megalithic culture. In fact, there is no evidence whatsoever that the Shetlanders were ever influenced by Megalithic culture at all. Neither did the culture spread to the Faroe Islands, some 220 miles to the northwest. The oldest evi-dence for human habitation here is at Kvívík, a municipality in the west of the island of Streymoy, where excavations have unearthed the remains of a Viking dwelling dating to around 1000 CE—4,000 years after the Megalithic age came to the British Isles.[7] The only other dry land in the North Sea, anywhere near where Fairland was, is Fair Isle—remarkably, the only part of Fairland to remain above sea level. Today, Fair Isle is a remote, treeless island, some 3 miles long and 2.5 miles wide, about

45 miles north of the Orkneys (and 25 miles south of the Shetlands), with a population of about 60 people. Seven thousand years ago, however, it had been an area of high moorland at the extreme north of Fairland.[8] As the only part of Fairland to still survive, is there any evidence of a civilization or sophisticated early culture on Fair Isle? What have archaeologists discovered here?

Not surprisingly, no evidence of sizable Neolithic settlements has been found on Fair Isle. When it was part of Fairland, the island had been a windswept upland, not the kind of place to establish a large community; if such settlements existed on Fairland, they would most likely have been in the lowlands. Nevertheless, the stone foundations of small clusters of oval-shaped stone building have been found at several locations on Fair Isle—for example, at Eas Brecks,[9] Vaasetter,[10] Pund,[11] and Shirva,[12] which, based on animal bone fragments found at the sites, have been dated to between 4000 and 3000 BCE. One such hut cluster is of particular interest. Between 1996 and 1997, excavations conducted by a team from Birmingham University at a site of an Iron Age promontory fort, above the bay of South Haven on the eastern side of the island, uncovered the foundations of three much earlier buildings, within which they discovered multiple fragments of grooved ware pottery dated to between 4000 and 3500 BCE.[13] Of course, such ceramics could have been traded from the Orkney Islands, but it's possible that the people who lived or worked here represented the last direct vestiges of a civilization that existed on Fairland. Besides the grooved ware pottery, another indication of Megalithic culture found on Fair Isle is an alignment of standing stones. Near the hut cluster at Eas Breck there still survives an alignment of 12 monoliths, which stand in a row about 425 feet long.[14] Unfortunately, the remoteness of Fair Isle has meant that no modern archaeological work has been conducted to establish its age. However, the stone alignment is remarkably like megalithic stone rows found throughout England, such as on Dartmoor in the south, the Lake

District in the north, and in northern Scotland.[15] There are also several isolated standing stones, such as a 5-foot monolith between Reeva and Lower Stonybreck in the southern part of the island.[16]

The existence of grooved ware pottery and a stone alignment on Fair Isle are tantalizing, but unfortunately these are far from proof that there was a Megalithic civilization throughout Fairland since such vestiges might be explained by migrants from the Orkney Islands. So what other clues exist?

One such mysterious archaeological feature has been termed a *burnt mound*. These are found on Fair Isle but not found on the Orkneys, and the concept might have originated on Fairland. A burnt mound is an archaeological feature consisting of a pile of charred and broken stones, which long ago were soot-blackened by prehistoric fires. The stones of metalworking furnaces and pottery kilns would eventually break due to repeated heating and cooling, and ultimately these would be discarded nearby to form the burnt mounds. Neolithic, Bronze Age, and Iron Age burnt mounds are common throughout the British Isles and elsewhere.[17] But the burnt mounds on Fair Isle are different, as no evidence of prehistoric kilns or furnaces are found in their vicinity. These unusual burnt mounds—of which there are around a dozen—are found beside the foundations of what had been small, isolated huts, erected close to the clusters of dwellings, such as at Vaasetter,[18] Shirva,[19] and Pund.[20] At the center of the hut foundations are the remains of a stone trough, showing indications that it was once lined with clay, enabling it to hold water. Beside the troughs are the telltale remains of circular hearths, nothing like kilns or furnaces that would, in any case, have been situated outside of buildings due to their extreme heat. Interestingly, most of these huts are sited next to natural springs, a source of running water. Scientific analysis of these Fair Isle burnt mound deposits have suggested that the stones hadn't cooled gradually, as would be expected for a kiln or furnace, but had shattered rapidly after having cold water poured over them. Although it has proved difficult to date the Fair Isle burnt mounds, archaeologists believe that this anomaly, together with the nearby supply of water and the small, one-room buildings containing a hearth and a water-holding trough, might be evidence of the world's earliest known saunas.[21] Stones may have been heated in the hearth and then had cold water from the trough poured over them to create steam. The small groups of dwellings, together with the nearby saunas (if that's what they were) and natural springs, on what is now Fair Isle, might be evidence that what was once an upland promontory at the north end of Fairland might have been a prehistoric spa resort.

So, what can we speculate about an ancient civilization that might have existed on Fairland over 6,000 years ago? They probably built stone circles, megalithic complexes, and monolithic alignments well before these appeared in the British Isles. And judging by what we find in the

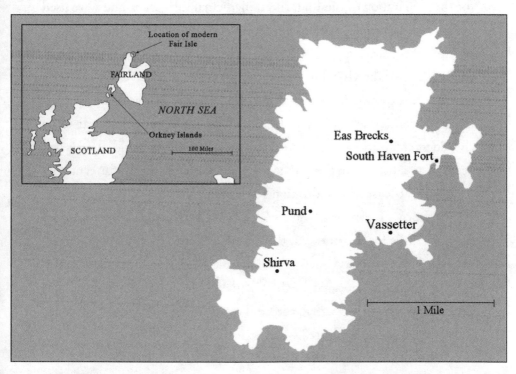

Fig. 10.1. Fair Isle and its location on what was once Fairland.

Orkneys, their dwellings may have been far more sophisticated than anything that would appear in the British Isles for centuries to come. Considering the passage tombs that suddenly appeared at the start of the Megalithic age, not to mention the skills needed to create the remarkable megalithic complexes and other Neolithic monuments, the Fairlanders might have had building technology years ahead of the time—perhaps the most advanced in all the contemporary world. The abrupt appearance of grooved ware pottery in the Orkneys suggests that a civilization on Fairland had the most sophisticated pottery in Europe, while the burnt mounds on Fair Isle imply that they could also have invented the sauna. And the contents of the enigmatic box tombs have revealed a people with an astonishingly advanced pharmaceutical knowledge for the time— again, something that appears abruptly and may well have originally been developed on Fairland. Moreover, it seems that stone circles were erected for the preparation of these advanced medicinal substances and were used as accurate celestial calendars to determine the intricate timing neces- sary for the cultivation of effective medicinal compounds. Other than the builders of the Göbekli Tepe monuments in Turkey (c. 9000 BCE), which seems to have been a localized anomaly, the Fairland culture, dat- ing from perhaps around 7000 BCE, maybe earlier, would appear to be the oldest civilization so far discovered anywhere in the world. And it was years in advance of anything that originated anywhere else for centuries to come—at least any civilization for which we have yet found conclu- sive evidence. (The people who built Göbekli Tepe certainly had complex building skills for the time, but there is no evidence they made pottery— they used stone-carved vessels—let alone the kind of sophisticated ceram- ics that suddenly appeared in the Orkneys. Moreover, no evidence has been found that they ever had the kind of advanced medicinal knowledge found in Megalithic culture.)

Who exactly might the Fairland people have been? Were they an offshoot of an advanced civilization from elsewhere, or could their culture have been completely home-grown? DNA extracted from prehistoric human remains shows that between the end of the last Ice Age and about 6,000 years ago the inhabitants of the British Isles were a single, closely related population: Mesolithic hunter-gatherers who differ genetically from their contemporaries in Europe and Scandinavia. Then, around 4000 BCE, a new people from the Iberian Peninsula (now Spain and Portugal) migrated along the North Atlantic coast to arrive in the British Isles by 3600 BCE. These were the early farmers who built the long barrows and dolmen tombs (p. 124–127), the so-called Barrow culture who by 3000 BCE had pretty much interbred with the earlier population. They became a single populace that we have been referring to as the Neolithic people, the inhabitants of the British Isles before the influx of the Beaker culture from the Netherlands around 2600 BCE. Fascinatingly, however, scientific examination of human remains found in the Orkney Islands dating from around 3000 BCE— when the Megalithic culture first appeared elsewhere in the British Isles—has revealed that the Orcadian population appears to have been the same as the earlier Mesolithic people.[22] In other words, the Neolithic newcomers from the Iberian Peninsula never migrated to the Orkneys.

Scientific analysis has found no DNA representative of the Neolithic people from the mainland British Isles evident among the Orkney Islanders until much later than 3000 BCE—centuries after they were starting to use groove ware pottery, create passage tombs, and build stone circles and megalithic complexes. This has been seen as supporting the now generally accepted theory that Megalithic culture existed on the Orkney Islands before the mainland British Isles. If Megalithic culture had originated with Neolithic migrants from the mainland British Isles, then we should expect to find evidence of their DNA in Orcadian human remains much earlier. DNA profiling of the inhabitants of Europe and Scandinavia around 4000 BCE has revealed a genetic melting pot of people originating in western Asia and the Mediterranean who had mingled freely since the ice retreated 6,000 years before. The exception was the Iberian Peninsula, where the inhabitants seem to have remained in relative isolation for millennia. The Iberians therefore had a unique genetic makeup that they brought with them when they migrated to the British Isles. Over the next millennium, until around 3000 BCE, the Iberians interbred with the native Mesolithic population, so that traces of their DNA can be found in most human remains of the mid to late Neolithic period throughout the British Isles. The exception here is the Orkney Islands, where human DNA is found to have been the same as the earlier early Neolithic British and Irish.

We have examined in detail how the Megalithic culture appeared abruptly on the Orkney Islands around 4000 BCE, meaning it must have developed over many centuries elsewhere. Yet there is no evidence of such a culture—with its monuments, burial practices, pottery, and pharmaceutical knowledge—anywhere else in the British Isles, mainland Europe, or Scandinavia, before it appeared on the Orkneys. As we find only early Neolithic DNA among the Orcadians before and immediately after 3000 BCE—the same as we find in the earlier, pre-Iberian British Isles—then, if the Megalithic know-how did come to the Orkneys with migrants from elsewhere, they must surely have come from some no-longer-existing part of the British Isles. And there is only one such land known to have still existed just prior to the Megalithic culture's first appearance on the Orkney Islands: Fairland. If the Fairlanders only had early Neolithic DNA, then they were probably the same as the original, post–Ice Age people of the British Isles, those who crossed the Doggerland land bridge from mainland Europe before 7000 BCE. Any Fairland civilization, therefore, would appear to have been home-grown, developed in isolation over centuries, and arising millennia before the civilizations of Egypt, Sumer, and the Indus Valley.

Staying with ancient DNA analysis, what is particularly interesting is what we find in the Megalithic box tombs found throughout the

British Isles, which seem to have been reserved for the burial of an elite group connected to the stone circles. Judging by the pots containing pharmaceutical substances buried with them, these elites were, perhaps among other things, the healers who used the stone circles to time the cultivation, harvesting, and preparation of medicinal extracts from the various parts of plants (see chapter 9). DNA analysis of human remains found in various box tombs located throughout England, Ireland, Scotland, and Wales—such as Haco's Tombs in North Ayrshire,[23] Bant's Carn on the Isles of Scilly,[24] and at Fingal's Cauldron on Scotland's Isle of Arran[25]—have revealed that those interred there were directly descended from the early Neolithic people who inhabited the British Isles before the arrival of the Iberians. As there is absolutely no indication that the inhabitants of the British Isles had any of the trappings of Megalithic culture until around 3000 BCE, then these high-status individuals could well have been the descendants of those who brought the Megalithic culture to these islands—either the Orcadians, or possibly the Fairlanders themselves.

The final question is: What might have become of the inhabitants of Fairland? It is quite clear that there was no mass exodus from Fairland in the buildup to 4000 BCE, when the last parts of the island were being inundated by the sea. If there were, we would expect to see evidence of a population increase in the British Isles, which we certainly don't. The population on Britain, for instance, is estimated to have been around 250,000 after the arrival of the Neolithic people from Iberia around 4000 BCE, when the first signs of Megalithic culture appear on the Orkneys. There is no indication of any significant increase until the arrival of the Beaker people around 2600 BCE.[26] What about the Orkney Islands? Few human remains have been found predating the Megalithic period, suggesting the population was low. Then, just as suddenly as the Megalithic culture appears, around 4000 BCE, the population seems to have significantly increased. It is not known exactly how many people lived on the Orkneys from this time, but judging by the number of tombs, settlements, and considerable evidence of prehistoric farming, it must have been substantially more than had lived there before. Considering the sheer size of the Bay of Firth megalithic complex—one of the largest yet known—the population of the Orkney Islands must have been about the size of the tribal population served by the similar-size complex at Stanton Drew in Somerset—perhaps around 10,000.[27] As the previous population appears to have been so much smaller, it is quite possible that most of these people were not merely the previous inhabits who had adopted Megalithic culture, but were the descendants of the Fairlanders themselves.

From what we have examined, the first postglacial people to settle Fairland would seem to have been one and the same as those who settled the rest of the British Isles before the Doggerland land bridge was submerged by around 7000 BCE. At present, however, we have no idea when Megalithic culture might first have evolved on the island. From the dating of discoveries off the coast of the Orkney Islands and on Fair Isle we can guess that the Fairland civilization must have existed before 4000 BCE. We can also surmise that it is unlikely to have existed before 6200 BCE. As we saw in chapter 2, the last of the Storegga Slides, a series of truly enormous landslides on the coast of Norway, caused a massive megatsunami that crossed 3,500 miles of the Atlantic at an estimated 400 miles an hour to thrash the eastern seaboard of North America with a wave over 100 feet high. And the carbon dating of ancient plant material deposited by the tsunami reveals that the wave traveled at least 50 miles inland. Such a tidal wave would have pounded Fairland far more violently. The coast of North America is 3,000 miles away, but Fairland is less than 400 miles from the gargantuan slide. The Storegga Slides would almost certainly have pulverized all but the highland regions of the island, including most human settlements. If any civilization had developed by this time, it would certainly have been wiped out. So, a reasonable guess would be that the Fairland civilization developed sometime after this, between 6000 and 5000 BCE, with new early Neolithic arrivals from the south. Then, by 4500 BCE, sea levels started rising when isostatic adjustment ceased. It is difficult to determine when the Bay of Firth megalithic complex was built, but we can assume it was just prior to 4000 BCE. Maybe sometime around then the Fairlanders disembarked for the Orkneys. But, as we have seen, there was no massive influx of people into the British Isles at the time—merely, perhaps, a few thousand into the Orkney Islands. Accordingly, not many Fairlanders would seem to have been left alive by 4000 BCE. By the end of the fifth millennium BCE, Fairland had been gradually sinking for some five centuries, and only the highlands would have remained. Yet, as there is no evidence of Megalithic culture appearing anywhere until it arrived on the Orkney Islands just prior to 4000 BCE, there seems nowhere else the Fairlanders could have gone. If the Megalithic culture did originate with a civilization on Fairland, as we have surmised, then its population must have been severely diminished before this time. But how?

Just over 6,000 years ago, parts of northern Canada were still covered by permanent ice. As with the earlier Storegga and Greenland landslides, streams from melting glaciers had carried trillions of tons of sediment to the edge of the west Canadian ice shelf. Somewhere around 4500 BCE, a massive underwater landslide on the coast of what is now Baffin Island caused another gigantic tidal wave to surge across the north Atlantic, this time from west to east. From plant material discovered in sediment deposits on the west coast of Scotland, it is estimated that the area was hit by a huge tsunami, as much as 50 feet high, traveling many miles inland.[28] This would almost certainly have pulverized the lower-lying areas of Fairland. This dreadful catastrophe might have brought any civilization on Fairland to its knees, only surviving on higher land. Perhaps it struggled on for a few more years before leaving for the Orkney Islands, where the last of the Fairlanders built a new Megalithic complex in what is now the Bay of Firth. Throughout the fourth millennium BCE, their descendants may have been the very Orcadians who enjoyed an isolated Megalithic way of life, until they traveled south around 3000 BCE when resources became depleted. There they shared their knowledge with the people of the British Isles, perhaps becoming the venerated healers and advisers buried in the enigmatic box tombs, the last descendants of a lost civilization, to be remembered only in the dim shadows of myths and legend.

Notes

CHAPTER 1.
A FORGOTTEN CIVILIZATION

1. *The Scotsman,* "Stone Circle to Rival Ring of Brodgar Found Off Orkney Coast."
2. Hoare, "Archaeology Breakthrough."
3. Mithen, *After the Ice.*
4. Macalister, *Lebor gabála Érenn.*
5. *The Book of Druimm Snechta,* probably written during the fifth century by early Christian missionaries, is cited as a source by the authors of many important early Irish manuscripts—for example, the *Book of the Dun Cow,* the *Book of Leinster,* the *Book of Ballymote,* and *the Great Book of Lecan.*
6. Dicuil, *Liber de Mensura Orbis Terrae* (Concerning the measurement of the world).
7. Unfortunately, Pytheas's *On the Ocean* does not survive in its entirety. However, excerpts and quotations from it are preserved in the works of later Roman-era authors such as Pliny the Elder, Strabo, and Diodorus of Sicily.
8. Evans and Berggren, *Geminos's Introduction to the Phenomena.*
9. Roller, *The Geography of Strabo.*
10. Mela, *De Situ Orbis.*
11. Avienus, *Ora Maritima.*
12. Pliny the Elder, *Natural History,* trans. Healey.
13. Procopius, *History of the Wars,* trans. Dewing.
14. Tacitus, *The Agricola and the Germania,* trans. Mattingly and Rivers.

15. McDonough, Prior, and Stansbury, *Servius' Commentary on Book Four of Virgil's Aeneid.*
16. Martínez and Salanova, *The Bell Beaker Transition in Europe.*
17. Parker-Pearson, *Bronze Age Britain.*
18. Darvill, *Prehistoric Britain.*
19. Barber, *Bronze and the Bronze Age.*
20. Bruck, *Bronze Age Landscapes.*
21. Henderson, *The Atlantic Iron Age.*
22. Cunliffe, *The Ancient Celts.*
23. For a full discussion of the continuation of Megalithic culture and the history of the Druids, see my book *Wisdomkeepers of Stonehenge.*
24. Holland, *Haunted Wales.*
25. Powell, "The Gold Ornament from Mold, Flintshire, North Wales."
26. Underwood, *Where the Ghosts Walk.*
27. Spier, Kroeber, and R. Lowie, *Klamath Ethnography.*
28. Bacon, and Lanphere, "Eruptive History and Geochronology of Mount Mazama and the Crater Lake Region, Oregon."

CHAPTER 2.
FIRST CITIES AND THE LEGEND
OF ATLANTIS

1. Maisels, *Early Civilizations of the Old World.*
2. Sparks, et al., *Digging up Jericho.*
3. Hodder, *Çatalhöyük.*
4. Chang, *The Archaeology of Ancient China.*
5. Akkermans, ed. *Excavations at Tell Sabi Abyad.*
6. Yoffee and Clark, *Early Stages in the Evolution of Mesopotamian Civilization.*
7. Chapman, *The Vinca Culture of South-east Europe.*
8. McGrail, *Boats of the World.*
9. Cooper and Hutchinson, *Plato.*
10. Lamb, *Plato in Twelve Volumes, Vol. 9.*
11. Phillips, *Act of God.*
12. Collins, *Gateway to Atlantis.*
13. Cooper and Hutchinson, *Plato.*
14. Shorey, *Plato in Twelve Volumes, Vols. 5 & 6.*
15. Cooper and Hutchinson, *Plato.*

16. Cooper and Hutchinson, *Plato.*
17. Lamb, *Plato in Twelve Volumes, Vol. 9.*
18. Evelyn-White, *Hesiod.*
19. Pliny the Elder, *Natural History,* trans. Healey.
20. Ovid, *Metamorphoses,* trans. Raeburn.
21. Herodotus, *The Histories,* trans. de Sélincourt.
22. Stanley, *Geological Evolution of the Mediterranean Basin.*
23. Bondevik, et al., "Record-breaking Height for 8000-Year-Old Tsunami in the North Atlantic."
24. Henrikson, *Geological History of Greenland.*
25. Michard, et al., *Continental Evolution.*

CHAPTER 3.
LOST CONTINENTS

1. Le Plongeon, *Sacred Mysteries among the Maya and the Quiché.*
2. Coe, *The Maya.*
3. Salisbury, *The Mayas, the Sources of Their History.*
4. De Bourbourg and Sainson, *The Manuscript Hunter.*
5. Desmond, *Yucatan through Her Eyes.*
6. Freidel and Schele, *A Forest of Kings.*
7. Miller and Taube, *An Illustrated Dictionary of the Gods and Symbols of Ancient Mexico and the Maya.*
8. Harasta and River, *Chichen Itza.*
9. Harastaand River, *Chichen Itza.*
10. Harasta and River, *Chichen Itza.*
11. Harasta and River, *Chichen Itza.*
12. Coe, *The Maya.*
13. Roys, *The Book of Chilam Balam of Chumayel.*
14. Tedlock, *Popol Vuh.*
15. Desmond, *Yucatan through Her Eyes.*
16. Donnelly, *Atlantis.*
17. Churchward, *The Lost Continent of Mu.*
18. Churchward, *The Lost Continent of Mu.*
19. Rossini, *Egyptian Hieroglyphics.*
20. Miller and Taube, *An Illustrated Dictionary of the Gods and Symbols of Ancient Mexico and the Maya.*

21. Wilkinson, *The Rise and Fall of Ancient Egypt*.
22. Coe, *The Maya*.
23. Singh, *Ancient India*.
24. Juneja, *Architecture in Medieval India*.
25. Grant-Peterkin, *A Companion to Easter Island*.
26. Roys, *The Book of Chilam Balam of Chumayel*.
27. Tedlock, *Popol Vuh*.
28. Pool, *Olmec Archaeology and Early Mesoamerica*.
29. Voorhies and Kennett, "Buried Sites on the Soconusco Coastal Plain, Chiapas, Mexico."
30. Pool, *Olmec Archaeology and Early Mesoamerica*.
31. Diehl and Daniel, *The Olmecs*.
32. Pool, *Olmec Archaeology and Early Mesoamerica*.
33. Magaña, *The Madrid Codex*.
34. Vail and Aveni, eds. *Madrid Codex*.
35. Blavatsky, *The Secret Doctrine*.
36. Chatterjee, Scotese, and Bajpai, *The Restless Indian Plate and Its Epic Voyage from Gondwana to Asia*.
37. Ramaswamy, *The Lost Land of Lemuria*.
38. Chaturvedi, *Skanda Purana*.
39. Ramaswamy, *The Lost Land of Lemuria*.

CHAPTER 4.
THE GREAT FLOOD

1. Kramer, *The Sumerians*.
2. Crawford, *Sumer and the Sumerians*.
3. Dalley, trans. *Myths from Mesopotamia Creation, The Flood, Gilgamesh, and Others*.
4. Crawford, *Sumer and the Sumerians*.
5. Matsumoto, "Preliminary Report on the Excavations at Kish."
6. Rose, "New Light on Human Prehistory in the Arabo-Persian Gulf Oasis."
7. Spencer, *Early Egypt*.
8. Romer and Budge, *The Egyptian Book of the Dead*.
9. Castlemon, *The Pyramid Texts*.
10. Stanley, "Nile Silt Yields Secret of Egyptian Civilization."
11. Possehl, *The Harappan Civilization*.

12. Krishnan, *Origin of Vedas.*
13. Bhatt, *The Satapatha Brahmana.*
14. Kenoyer, *Ancient Cities of the Indus Valley Civilization.*
15. Coppa, et al., "Early Neolithic Tradition of Dentistry."
16. Athar, et al., "Distribution of Surface Sediments off Indus Delta on the Continental Shelf of Pakistan."
17. Ferrier, et al., "Sea-Level Responses to Erosion and Deposition of Sediment in the Indus River Basin and the Arabian Sea."
18. Kenoyer, *Ancient Cities of the Indus Valley Civilization.*
19. Yang, Deming, and Turner, *Handbook of Chinese Mythology.*
20. Baxter and Sagart, *Old Chinese.*
21. Loewe and Shaughnessy, *The Cambridge History of Ancient China.*
22. Liu, *The Chinese Neolithic.*
23. Guo and Wen, *China's Major Archaeological Discovery.*
24. Gen 6–9 (KJV).
25. Gen 8:4 (KJV).
26. George, *The Epic of Gilgamesh.*
27. Dimitrov and Dimitrov, *The Black Sea, The Flood, and the Ancient Myths.*
28. Dimitrov and Dimitrov, *The Black Sea, The Flood, and the Ancient Myths.*
29. Hoena, *Cleansing the World.*
30. Bauman, *Earth's Water Cycle.*
31. Suh, ed. *Leonardo's Notebooks.*
32. Mayor, *The First Fossil Hunters.*

CHAPTER 5.
MELTING ICE, CLIMATE CHANGE, AND PANDEMICS

1. Fagan, *The Complete Ice Age.*
2. Jha, *The Water Book.*
3. Steele, *Ocean Currents.*
4. Major and Cook, *Ancient China.*
5. Collins, *Göbekli Tepe.*
6. Burroughs, *Climate Change in Prehistory.*
7. Brown, "How Microbes Survive in Freezing Conditions."
8. Miner, Edwards, and Miller, "Deep Frozen Arctic Microbes Are Waking Up."
9. Martin, and Goodman, "Health Conditions before Columbus."

10. Smith, "Counting the Dead."

11. Ezhova, et al., "Climatic Factors Influencing the Anthrax Outbreak of 2016 in Siberia, Russia."

12. Liverpool, "A Deadly Seal Virus May Be Spreading Faster due to Melting Arctic Ice."

13. Martin, *Twilight of the Mammoths*.

14. Payo, *What Killed the Mammoths?*

15. Snook, *Ice Age Extinction*.

16. Rascovan, et al., "Emergence and Spread of Basal Lineages of *Yersinia Pestis* During the Neolithic Decline."

17. Ellis, "The Cucuteni–Tripolye Culture."

18. Gronenborn, et al., "Adaptive Cycles and Climate Fluctuations."

19. Knitter, et al., "Transformations and Site Locations from a Landscape Archaeological Perspective."

20. Stilborg, "Regionality in the Study of the Ertebolle Culture."

21. Whittle, *Europe in the Neolithic*.

22. Dengler, "Scientists Discovered the Oldest Human Plague."

23. Rascovan, et al., "Emergence and Spread of Basal Lineages of *Yersinia Pestis* During the Neolithic Decline."

CHAPTER 6.
THE MYSTERIES OF THE MEGALITHIC CULTURE

1. Gaffney, Thomson, and Finch, *Mapping Doggerland*.

2. Toghill, *Geology of Britain*.

3. Wickham-Jones, Dawson, and Bates, "Drowned Stone Age Settlement of the Bay of Firth, Orkney, Scotland."

4. Phillips, *Wisdomkeepers of Stonehenge*.

5. Reid, *Prehistoric Houses in Britain*.

6. Pollard, *Neolithic Britain*.

7. Foster, *Maeshowe and the Heart of Neolithic Orkney*.

8. Renfrew, *The Prehistory of Orkney*.

9. Martínez and Salanova, *The Bell Beaker Transition in Europe*.

10. Thomas, *Understanding the Neolithic*.

11. Malone, *Neolithic Britain and Ireland*.

12. Henderson, *The Atlantic Iron Age*.

13. Weir, *Early Ireland*.

14. Duling, *Carbon Dating*.

15. Richards and Britton, eds., *Archaeological Science*.

16. Richards and Britton, eds., *Archaeological Science*.

17. Thom, *Megalithic Remains in Britain and Brittany*.

18. Tilley, *An Ethnography of the Neolithic*.

CHAPTER 7.
STONE CIRCLES, EARTHWORKS, AND STANDING STONES

1. Martínez and Salanova, *The Bell Beaker Transition in Europe*.

2. Darvill, *Prehistoric Britain*.

3. Burl, *Prehistoric Avebury*.

4. Leary, *Silbury Hill*.

5. Pitts and Whittle, "The Development and Date of Avebury."

6. Wainwright, *Durrington Walls*.

7. Gaffney, et al.,"The Stonehenge Hidden Landscapes Project."

8. Hawkins, *Stonehenge Decoded*.

9. Bayliss, Bronk-Ramsey, and MacCormac, "Dating Stonehenge."

10. Strong, *Stanton Drew and Its Ancient Stone Circles*.

11. Burl, *The Stone Circles of the British Isles*.

12. Ritchie, *The Stones of Stenness, Orkney*.

13. Wickham-Jones, Dawson, and Bates, "Drowned Stone Age Settlement of the Bay of Firth, Orkney, Scotland."

14. Burl, *The Stone Circles of the British Isles*.

15. Byng, *Dartmoor's Mysterious Megaliths*.

16. Ray, *The Archaeology of Herefordshire*.

17. Barber and Williams, *The Ancient Stones of Wales*.

18. Ross, *Ancient Scotland*.

CHAPTER 8.
MEGALITHIC CIVILIZATION

1. Smith and Brickley, *People of the Long Barrows*.

2. Smith and Brickley, *People of the Long Barrows*.

3. Smithand Brickley *People of the Long Barrows*.

4. Malone, *Neolithic Britain and Ireland*.

5. Wickham-Jones, *Monuments of Orkney*.

6. Foster, *Maeshowe and the Heart of Neolithic Orkney*.

7. Foster, *Maeshowe and the Heart of Neolithic Orkney*.

8. Lee, "Banks Chambered Tomb, South Ronaldsay, Orkney Excavation."

9. Stout and Stout, *Newgrange*.

10. Lynch, *Prehistoric Anglesey*.

11. Lynch, *Prehistoric Anglesey*.

12. Smith and Brickley, *People of the Long Barrows*.

13. Malone, *Neolithic Britain and Ireland*.

14. Barber, *Prehistoric Textiles*.

15. Cleal and MacSween, *Grooved Ware in Great Britain and Ireland*.

16. Hunt, *The Oxford Handbook of Archaeological Ceramic Analysis*.

17. Cleal and MacSween, *Grooved Ware in Great Britain and Ireland*.

18. Ritchie, *Prehistoric Orkney*.

19. Ritchie, *Prehistoric Orkney*.

20. Clarke, *Skara Brae*.

21. Reid, *Prehistoric Houses in Britain*.

22. Wickham-Jones, *Monuments of Orkney*.

23. Clarke, *Skara Brae*.

24. Wickham-Jones, *Orkney*.

25. McGrail, *Ancient Boats and Ships*.

CHAPTER 9.
GEOMANCERS AND HEALERS

1. Watkins, *The Old Straight Track*.

2. Michell, *The View Over Atlantis*.

3. Schmieke, *The Origin of Feng Shui*.

4. Hadingham, *Lines to the Mountain Gods*.

5. Novak, *Christianity and the Roman Empire*.

6. Graves, *Needles of Stone*.

7. Hawkins, *Stonehenge Decoded*.

8. Magli, *Archaeoastronomy*.

9. Magli, *Archaeoastronomy*.

10. Shore-Henshall, *The Chambered Tombs of Scotland*.

11. Shore-Henshall, *The Chambered Tombs of Scotland*.

12. Ashbee, "Excavations at Halangy Down, St Mary's, Scilly."

13. Barnatt, *Barrows in the Peak District.*

14. Britnell and Savoury, *Gwernvale and Penywyrlod.*

15. Armstrong, *Yellowmead Stone Circles, Sheepstor.*

16. Shore-Henshall, *The Chambered Tombs of Scotland.*

17. Clare, *Prehistoric Monuments of the Lake District.*

18. Ashmore, *Calanais.*

19. Morgan and Morgan, *Prehistoric Cheshire.*

20. Rowlands, *Mona Antiqua Restaurata.*

21. Renfrew, *The Prehistory of Orkney.*

22. Chiasson, et al., "Acaricidal Properties of *Artemisia absinthium* and *Tanacetum vulgare.*"

23. Sequin, *The Chemistry of Plants.*

24. Soni, et al., "Pharmacological Properties of *Datura stramonium.*"

25. Bown, *The Royal Horticultural Society New Encyclopedia of Herbs and Their Uses.*

26. Sequin, *The Chemistry of Plants.*

27. Livarda, Madgwick, and Mora, *The Bioarchaeology of Ritual and Religion.*

28. Sequin, *The Chemistry of Plants.*

29. Sequin, *The Chemistry of Plants.*

CHAPTER 10.
FAIRLAND

1. Gaffney, Thomson, and Finch, *Mapping Doggerland.*

2. Toghill, *Geology of Britain.*

3. Turner, *Ancient Shetland.*

4. Fojut, *Prehistoric and Viking Shetland.*

5. Turner, *Ancient Shetland.*

6. Copper, et al., "Tracing the Lines."

7. Wylie, *The Faroe Islands.*

8. Gaffney, Thomson, and Finch, *Mapping Doggerland.*

9. Hunter, *Fair Isle Survey: Interim 1985.*

10. Hunter, *Fair Isle Survey: Interim 1987.*

11. Hunter, *Fair Isle Survey: Interim 1984.*

12. Hunter, *Fair Isle Survey: Interim 1984.*

13. Lamb, "Iron Age Promontory Forts in the Northern Isles."

14. Hunter, *Fair Isle Survey: Interim 1985.*

15. Scarre, *The Megalithic Monuments of Britain and Ireland*.

16. Hunter, *Fair Isle Survey: Interim 1984*.

17. Ó Néill, *Burnt Mounds in Northern and Western Europe*.

18. Hunter, *Fair Isle Survey: Interim 1984*.

19. Hunter, *Fair Isle Survey: Interim 1984*.

20. Hunter, *Fair IsleSsurvey: Interim 1984*.

21. Doughton, *Reinterpreting the Burnt Mounds of Shetland*.

22. Shennan, *The First Farmers of Europe*.

23. Humble, "Haco's Tomb Chambered Cairn."

24. Sawyer, *Isles of the Dead?*

25. Bradley, et al., *Stages and Screens*.

26. Thomas, *The Birth of Neolithic Britain*.

27. David, "Stanton Drew."

28. Williams, "Skimming the Surface of Underwater Landslides."

Bibliography

Akkermans, Peter, ed. *Excavations at Tell Sabi Abyad.* Oxford, UK: BAR Publishing, 1989.

Armstrong, Kayt. *Yellowmead Stone Circles, Sheepstor.* Okehampton, UK: Edgemoor Publishing, 2009.

Ashbee, Paul. "Excavations at Halangy Down, St Mary's, Scilly." *Cornish Archaeology* 9 (1970).

Ashmore, Patrick. *Calanais: The Standing Stones.* Edinburgh, UK: Historic Scotland, 2002.

Athar, Ali Khan, et al. "Distribution of Surface Sediments off Indus Delta on the Continental Shelf of Pakistan." *Pakistan Journal of Marine Sciences* 2 (1993).

Avienus, R. Festus. *Ora Maritima.* Whitefish, Mont.: Kessinger Publishing, 2010.

Bacon, Charles R., and Marvin A. Lanphere. "Eruptive History and Geochronology of Mount Mazama and the Crater Lake Region, Oregon." *Geological Society of America Bulletin* 118 (2006).

Barber, Chris, and John Godfrey Williams. *The Ancient Stones of Wales.* Llanfoist, UK: Blorenge Books, 1989.

Barber, E. *Prehistoric Textiles.* Princeton, N.J.: Princeton University Press, 1993.

Barber, Martyn. *Bronze and the Bronze Age.* Stroud, UK: The History Press, 2002.

Barnatt, J. *Barrows in the Peak District.* Sheffield, UK: J. R. Collis Publications, 1996.

Bauman, Amy. *Earth's Water Cycle.* Milwaukee, Wisc.: Gareth Stevens Publishing, 2007.

Baxter, William, and Laurent Sagart. *Old Chinese: A New Reconstruction.* Oxford, UK: Oxford University Press, 2014.

Bayliss, A., C. Bronk-Ramsey, and F. G. MacCormac. "Dating Stonehenge." *Proceedings of the British Academy* 92 (2016).

Bhatt, Jeet Ram. *The Satapatha Brahmana.* New Delhi: Eastern Book Linkers, 2009.

Blavatsky, H. P. *The Secret Doctrine.* Den Haag, Netherlands: Theosophical University Press, 1971.

Bondevik, Stein, Sue Dawson, Alastair Dawson, and Øystein Lohne. "Record-Breaking Height for 8000-Year-Old Tsunami in the North Atlantic." *Eos, Transactions, American Geophysical Union* 84 (2003).

Bown, Deni. *The Royal Horticultural Society New Encyclopedia of Herbs and Their Uses.* London: Dorling Kindersley, 1995.

Bradley, R. et al. *Stages and Screens: An Investigation of Four Henge Monuments in Northern and North-Eastern Scotland.* Edinburgh, UK: Society of Antiquaries of Scotland, 2011.

Britnell, W. J., and H. N. Savoury. *Gwernvale and Penywyrlod.* Carmarthen, UK: Cambrian Archaeological Association, 1984.

Brown, Paige. "How Microbes Survive in Freezing Conditions," *Science Daily* website, October 10, 2013.

Bruck, Joanna. *Bronze Age Landscapes: Tradition and Transformation.* Oxford, UK: Oxbow Books, 2002.

Burl, Aubrey. *Prehistoric Avebury.* New Haven, Conn.: Yale University Press, 2002.

Burl, Aubrey. *The Stone Circles of the British Isles.* New Haven, Conn.: Yale University Press, 1979.

Burroughs, William James. *Climate Change in Prehistory.* Cambridge, UK: Cambridge University Press, 2008.

Byng, Brian. *Dartmoor's Mysterious Megaliths.* Los Angeles: Barron Jay, 1979.

Castlemon, Harry. *The Pyramid Texts.* London: Forgotten Books, 2008.

Chang, Kwang-chih. *The Archaeology of Ancient China.* New Haven, Conn.: Yale University Press, 1986.

Chapman, John. *The Vinca Culture of South-east Europe.* Oxford, UK: BAR Publishing, 1981.

Chatterjee, Sankar, Christopher R. Scotese, and Sunil Bajpai. *The Restless Indian Plate and its Epic Voyage from Gondwana to Asia: Its Tectonic, Paleoclimatic, and Paleobiogeographic Evolution.* Boulder, Colo.: Geological Society of America, 2017.

Chaturvedi, B. K. *Skanda Purana*. New Delhi: Diamond Pocket Books, 2010.

Chiasson, Hélène, et al. "Acaricidal Properties of *Artemisia absinthium* and *Tanacetum vulgare* (Asteraceae) Essential Oils Obtained by Three Methods of Extraction." *Journal of Economic Entomology* 94 (2001).

Churchward, James. *The Lost Continent of Mu: Motherland of Man*. Whitefish, Mont.: Kessinger Publishing, 2010.

Clare, Tom. *Prehistoric Monuments of the Lake District*. Stroud, UK: The History Press, 2007.

Clarke, D. V. *Skara Brae: Northern Europe's Best Preserved Neolithic Village*. Edinburgh, UK: Historic Scotland, 2003.

Cleal, Rosamund, and Ann MacSween, eds. *Grooved Ware in Great Britain and Ireland*. Oxford, UK: Oxbow Books, 1999.

Coe, Michael, D. *The Maya*. London: Thames and Hudson, 2011.

Collins, Andrew. *Gateway to Atlantis: The Search for the Source of a Lost Civilization*. New York: Carroll & Graf, 2001.

Collins, Andrew. *Göbekli Tepe: Genesis of the Gods*. Rochester, Vt.: Bear & Company, 2014.

Cooper, John, and D. S. Hutchinson, eds., *Plato: Complete Works*. Cambridge, Mass.: Hackett, 1997.

Coppa, A., et al. "Early Neolithic Tradition of Dentistry." *Nature* 440 (2006).

Copper, Mike, Derek Hamilton, and Alex Gibson. "Tracing the Lines—Scottish Grooved Ware Trajectories Beyond Orkney." *Proceedings of the Society of Antiquaries of Scotland* 151 (2021).

Crawford, Harriet. *Sumer and the Sumerians*. Cambridge, UK: Cambridge University Press, 2004.

Cunliffe, Barry. *The Ancient Celts*. Oxford, UK: Oxford University Press, 1997.

Dalley, Stephanie, trans. *Myths from Mesopotamia Creation, The Flood, Gilgamesh, and Others*. Oxford, UK: Oxford University Press, 2008.

Darvill, Timothy. *Prehistoric Britain*. Abingdon, UK: Routledge, 2010.

David, Andrew. "Stanton Drew." *The Newsletter of the Prehistoric Society* 28 (1998).

De Bourbourg, Charles and Katia Sainson. *The Manuscript Hunter: Brasseur de Bourbourg's Travels through Central America and Mexico, 1854–1859*. Norman: University of Oklahoma Press, 2017.

Dengler, Roni. "Scientists Discovered the Oldest Human Plague. It Took Down Neolithic Farmers and Changed Europe's History." *Discover Magazine*, December, 2018.

Desmond, Lawrence. *Yucatan through Her Eyes: Alice Dixon Le Plongeon, Writer and Expeditionary Photographer.* Albuquerque: University of New Mexico Press, 2009.

Dicuil, James J. *Liber de Mensura Orbis Terrae* (Concerning the measurement of the world). Charleston, S.C.: Nabu Press, 2010.

Diehl, Richard A. and Glyn Daniel. *The Olmecs: America's First Civilization.* London: Thames and Hudson, 2006.

Dimitrov, Petko, and Dimitar Dimitrov. *The Black Sea, The Flood, and the Ancient Myths.* Varna, Bulgaria: Slavena, 2004.

Donnelly, Ignatius. *Atlantis: The Antediluvian World.* Scotts Valley, Calif.: CreateSpace Publishing, 2008.

Doughton, Lauren. *Reinterpreting the Burnt Mounds of Shetland.* Manchester, UK: Manchester University Press, 2014.

Duling, Kaitlyn. *Carbon Dating: Great Discoveries in Science.* New York: Cavendish Square Publishing, 2019.

Ellis, Linda. "The Cucuteni–Tripolye Culture: Study in Technology and the Origins of Complex Society." *British Archaeological Report* 217 (1984).

Evans, James, and J. Lennart Berggren. *Geminos's Introduction to the Phenomena: A Translation and Study of a Hellenistic Survey of Astronomy.* Princeton, N.J.: Princeton University Press, 2018.

Evelyn-White, Hugh G. *Hesiod: The Homeric Hymns and Homerica.* Cambridge, Mass.: Harvard University Press, 1914.

Ezhova, E., et al. "Climatic Factors Influencing the Anthrax Outbreak of 2016 in Siberia, Russia." *EcoHealth* 18 (2021).

Fagan, Brian. ed. *The Complete Ice Age: How Climate Change Shaped the World.* London: Thames and Hudson, 2009.

Ferrier, Ken, et al. "Sea-Level Responses to Erosion and Deposition of Sediment in the Indus River Basin and the Arabian Sea." *Earth and Planetary Science Letters* 416 (2015).

Fojut, Noel. *Prehistoric and Viking Shetland.* Lerwick, UK: Shetland Times Ltd., 2006.

Foster, Sally. *Maeshowe and the Heart of Neolithic Orkney.* Edinburgh, UK: Historic Scotland, 2006.

Freidel, David, and Linda Schele. *A Forest of Kings: The Untold Story of the Ancient Maya.* New York: William Morrow, 1992.

Gaffney, Chris, et al. "The Stonehenge Hidden Landscapes Project." *Archaeological Prospection* 19, no. 2 (2012).

Gaffney, Vincent, Kenneth Thomson, and Simon Finch, eds. *Mapping Doggerland: The Mesolithic Landscapes of the Southern North Sea.* Oxford, UK: Archaeopress, 2007.

George, Andrew. trans. *The Epic of Gilgamesh.* London: Penguin, 2002.

Gibson, Paul. *Prehistoric Pottery in Britain & Ireland.* Stroud, UK: The History Press, 2002.

Grant-Peterkin, James. *A Companion to Easter Island.* Self-Published, 2004.

Graves, Tom. *Needles of Stone.* Winnipeg, Canada: Turnstone, 1978.

Greenwell, William, and George Rolleston. *British Barrows: A Record of the Examination of Sepulchral Mounds in Various Parts of England.* Charleston, S.C.: Nabu Press, 2010.

Gronenborn, Detlef, Hans-Christoph Strien, Stephan Dietrich, and Frank Sirocko. "'Adaptive Cycles' and Climate Fluctuations: A Case Study from Linear Pottery Culture in Western Central Europe." *Journal of Archaeological Science* 51 (2014).

Guo, Jia, and Wu Ju Wen. *China's Major Archaeological Discovery.* Norwalk, Conn.: Heritage Press, 2014.

Hadingham, Evan. *Lines to the Mountain Gods: Nazca and the Mysteries of Peru.* Norman: University of Oklahoma Press, 1988.

Harasta, Jess, Charles and River. *Chichen Itza: The History and Mystery of the Maya's Most Famous City.* Scotts Valley, Calif.: CreateSpace Publishing, 2013.

Hawkins, Gerald. *Stonehenge Decoded.* London: Doubleday, 1965.

Henderson, Jon. *The Atlantic Iron Age: Settlement and Identity in the First Millennium BC.* Abingdon, UK: Routledge, 2007.

Henrikson, N. *Geological History of Greenland: Four Billion Years of Earth Evolution.* Copenhagen: GEUS, 2005.

Herodotus. *The Histories.* Translated by Aubrey de Sélincourt. London: Penguin, 2003.

Hoare, Callum. "Archaeology Breakthrough: How 'Genesis of Stonehenge' Was Found after Scottish Bay Scan." *The Express,* November 8, 2019.

Hodder, Ian. *Çatalhöyük: The Leopard's Tale.* London: Thames and Hudson, 2011.

Hoena, Blake. *Cleansing the World: Flood Myths Around the World.* North Mankato, Minn.: Capstone Press, 2017.

Holland, Richard. *Haunted Wales: A Guide to Welsh Ghostlore.* Stroud, UK: The History Press, 2011.

Humble, J. "Haco's Tomb Chambered Cairn." *Discovery and Excavation in Scotland* 16 (2015).

Hunt, Alice, ed. *The Oxford Handbook of Archaeological Ceramic Analysis.* Oxford, UK: Oxford University Press, 2016.

Hunter, J. R. ed. *Fair Isle Survey: Interim 1984.* Bradford, UK: Bradford University Press, 1984.

Hunter, J. R. ed. *Fair Isle Survey: Interim 1985.* Bradford, UK: Bradford University Press, 1985.

Hunter, J. R. ed. *Fair Isle Survey: Interim 1987.* Bradford, UK: Bradford University Press, 1987.

Jha, Alok. *The Water Book.* London Headline, 2015.

Juneja, Monica. *Architecture in Medieval India.* New Delhi: Permanent Black, 2002.

Kenoyer, Jonathan. *Ancient Cities of the Indus Valley Civilization.* Oxford, UK: Oxford University Press, 1998.

Knitter, Daniel, et al. "Transformations and Site Locations from a Landscape Archaeological Perspective: The Case of Neolithic Wagrien, Schleswig-Holstein, Germany." *Land Magazine* 8 (2019).

Kramer, Samuel Noah. *The Sumerians: Their History, Culture, and Character.* Chicago: University of Chicago Press, 1971.

Krishnan, K. S. *Origin of Vedas.* Chennai, India: Notion Press, 2019.

Lamb, R. G. "Iron Age Promontory Forts in the Northern Isles." *British Archaeological Report* 79 (1980).

Lamb, W. R. M. trans. *Plato in Twelve Volumes, Vol. 9.* Cambridge, Mass.: Harvard University Press, 1925.

Le Plongeon, Augustus. *Sacred Mysteries Among the Maya and the Quiché.* Neuilly, France: Ulan Press, 2012.

Leary, Jim. *Silbury Hill: The Largest Prehistoric Mound in Europe.* London: English Heritage, 2014.

Lee, D. "Banks Chambered Tomb, South Ronaldsay, Orkney excavation." *The Journal of Archaeology Scotland* 12 (2011).

Liu, Li. *The Chinese Neolithic: Trajectories to Early States.* Cambridge, UK: Cambridge University Press, 2008.

Livarda, Alexandra, Richard Madgwick, and Santiago Riera Mora, eds. *The Bioarchaeology of Ritual and Religion.* Oxford, UK: Oxbow Books, 2017.

Liverpool, Layla. "A Deadly Seal Virus May Be Spreading Faster due to Melting Arctic Ice." *New Scientist* 3256 (2019).

Loewe, Michael, and Edward Shaughnessy. *The Cambridge History of Ancient China: From the Origins of Civilization to 221 BC.* Cambridge, UK: Cambridge University Press, 1999.

Lynch, Frances. *Prehistoric Anglesey: The Archaeology of the Island to the Roman Conquest.* Llangefni, UK: Anglesey Antiquarian Society, 1991.

Macalister, Robert Alexander Stewart. *Lebor gabála Érenn: The book of the taking of Ireland.* Charleston, S.C:. Nabu Press, 2010.

Magaña, Daniel Castellanos. *The Madrid Codex.* Scotts Valley, Calif.: CreateSpace Publishing, 2018.

Magli, Giulio. *Archaeoastronomy: Introduction to the Science of Stars and Stones.* New York: Springer, 2015.

Maisels, Charles. *Early Civilizations of the Old World: The Formative Histories of Egypt, The Levant, Mesopotamia, India, and China.* Abingdon, UK: Routledge, 2003

Major, John S., and Constance A. Cook. *Ancient China.* Abingdon, UK: Routledge, 2016.

Malone, Caroline. *Neolithic Britain and Ireland.* Stroud, UK: The History Press, 2001.

Martin, Debra L., and Alan H. Goodman. "Health Conditions before Columbus: Paleopathology of Native North Americans." *Western Journal of Medicine* 176 (2002).

Martin, Paul S. *Twilight of the Mammoths: Ice Age Extinctions and the Rewilding of America.* Berkeley: University of California Press, 2007.

Martínez, Maria, and Laure Salanova, eds. *The Bell Beaker Transition in Europe.* Oxford, UK: Oxbow Books, 2015.

Matsumoto, K. "Preliminary Report on the Excavations at Kish." *Journal of Western Asiatic Studies* 12 (1991).

Mayor, Adrienne. *The First Fossil Hunters: Dinosaurs, Mammoths, and Myth in Greek and Roman Times.* Princeton, N.J.: Princeton University Press, 2011.

McDonough, Christopher Michael, Richard E. Prior, and Mark Stansbury, trans. *Servius' Commentary on Book Four of Virgil's "Aeneid": An Annotated Translation.* Mundelein, Ill.: Bolchazy-Carducci, 2002.

McGrail, Sean. *Ancient Boats and Ships.* London: Shire Books, 2006.

McGrail, Sean. *Boats of the World: From the Stone Age to Medieval Times.* Oxford, UK: Oxford University Press, 2004.

Mela, Pomponius. *De Situ Orbis.* Whitefish, Mont.: Kessinger Publishing, 2010.

Michard, A., O. Saddiqi, A. Chalouan, and D. Frizon de Lamotte, eds.

Continental Evolution: The Geology of Morocco. Berlin, Germany: Springer-Verlag, 2008.

Michell, John. *The View Over Atlantis*. New York: Ballantine Books, 1977.

Miller, Mary Ellen, and Karl Taube. *An Illustrated Dictionary of the Gods and Symbols of Ancient Mexico and the Maya*. London: Thames & Hudson, 1997.

Miner, Kimberley R., Arwyn Edwards, and Charles Miller. "Deep Frozen Arctic Microbes Are Waking Up." *Scientific American* 323 (2020).

Mithen, Steven. *After the Ice: A Global Human History, 20,000–5000 BC*. London: Weidenfeld & Nicolson, 2004.

Morgan, Victoria, and Paul Morgan. *Prehistoric Cheshire*. London: Landmark Publishing, 2004.

Novak, Ralph, M. *Christianity and the Roman Empire: Background Texts*. Manchester, UK: Trinity Press, 2001.

Ó Néill, John. *Burnt Mounds in Northern and Western Europe*. Saarbrücken, Germany: VDM Verlag, 2009.

Ovid. *Metamorphoses: A New Verse Translation*. Translated by David Raeburn. London: Penguin, 2004.

Parker-Pearson, Mike. *Bronze Age Britain*. London: Batsford, 2005.

Payo, Robert. *What Killed the Mammoths? Field Bulletin, January 2009*. Columbus: Ohio State University, 2009.

Phillips, Graham. *Act of God*. London: Sidgwick & Jackson, 1998.

Phillips, Graham. *Wisdomkeepers of Stonehenge*. Rochester, Vt.: Bear & Company, 2019.

Pitts, M., and A. Whittle. "The Development and Date of Avebury." *Proceedings of the Prehistoric Society* 58 (1992).

Pliny the Elder. *Natural History—A Selection*. Translated by John Healey. London: Penguin, 2004.

Pollard. Joshua. *Neolithic Britain*. London: Shire Books, 2002.

Pool, Christopher. *Olmec Archaeology and Early Mesoamerica*. Cambridge, UK: Cambridge University Press, 2007.

Possehl, Gregory L. *The Harappan Civilization*. Liverpool, UK. Liverpool University Press, 1982.

Powell, T. G. E. "The Gold Ornament from Mold, Flintshire, North Wales." *Proceedings of the Prehistoric Society* 19 (1953).

Procopius, *History of the Wars, Volume V*. Translated by H. B. Dewing. Cambridge, Mass.: Harvard University Press, 1928.

Ramaswamy, Sumathi. *The Lost Land of Lemuria: Fabulous Geographies, Catastrophic Histories.* Berkeley: University of California Press, 2005.

Rascovan, Nicolás, Kristian Kristiansen, Rasmus Nielsen, Eske Willerslev, Christelle Desnues, and Simon Rasmussen. "Emergence and Spread of Basal Lineages of *Yersinia Pestis* during the Neolithic Decline." *Cell* 176 (2019).

Ray, Keith. *The Archaeology of Herefordshire: An Exploration.* Little Logaston, UK: Logaston Press, 2015.

Reid, M. L. *Prehistoric Houses in Britain.* London: Shire Books, 1993.

Renfrew, Colin, ed. *The Prehistory of Orkney: 4000 BC–1000 AD.* Edinburgh, UK: Edinburgh University Press, 1987.

Richards, Michael, and Kate Britton, eds. *Archaeological Science: An Introduction.* Cambridge, UK: Cambridge University Press, 2020.

Ritchie, Anna. *Prehistoric Orkney.* London: Batsford, 1995.

Ritchie, Graham. *The Stones of Stenness, Orkney.* Edinburgh, UK: NMS Enterprises, 1997.

Roller, Duane W. *The Geography of Strabo: An English Translation, with Introduction and Notes.* Cambridge, UK: Cambridge University Press, 2014.

Romer, John, ed, E. A. Wallis Budge, trans. *The Egyptian Book of the Dead.* London: Penguin, 2008.

Rose, Jeffrey. "New Light on Human Prehistory in the Arabo-Persian Gulf Oasis." *Current Anthropology* 51 (2010).

Ross, Stewart. *Ancient Scotland.* New York: Barnes & Noble, 1991.

Rossini, Stephane. *Egyptian Hieroglyphics: How to Read and Write Them.* Mineola, N.Y.: Dover Publications, 1989.

Rowlands, Henry. *Mona Antiqua Restaurata.* Whitefish, Mont.: Kessinger Publishing, 2010.

Roys, Ralph L. *The Book of Chilam Balam of Chumayel.* London: Forgotten Books, 2008.

Salisbury, Stephen. *The Mayas, the Sources of Their History. Dr. Le Plongeon in Yucatan, His Account of Discoveries.* Wolverhampton, UK: Franklin Classics, 2018.

Sawyer, Katharine. *Isles of the Dead?: The Setting and Function of the Bronze Age Chambered Cairns and Cists of the Isles of Scilly.* Oxford, UK: Archaeopress, 2015.

Scarre, Chris. *The Megalithic Monuments of Britain and Ireland.* London: Thames & Hudson, 2007.

Schmieke, Marcus. *The Origin of Feng Shui.* Cardiff, UK: Goloka Books, 2002.

The Scotsman. "Stone Circle to Rival Ring of Brodgar Found Off Orkney Coast." October 19, 2011.

Sequin, Margareta. *The Chemistry of Plants: Perfumes, Pigments and Poisons.* London: Royal Society of Chemistry, 2015.

Shennan, S. *The First Farmers of Europe: An Evolutionary Perspective.* Cambridge, UK: Cambridge University Press, 2018.

Shore-Henshall, Audrey. *The Chambered Tombs of Scotland. Vol. 2.* Edinburgh, UK: Edinburgh University Press, 1972.

Shorey, Paul, trans. *Plato in Twelve Volumes, Vols. 5 & 6.* Cambridge, Mass.: Harvard University Press, 1969.

Singh, Upinder. *Ancient India: New Research.* Oxford, UK: Oxford University Press, 2010.

Smith, David Michael. "Counting the Dead: Estimating the Loss of Life in the Indigenous Holocaust, 1492–Present." Proceedings of the Twelfth Native American Symposium, Durant, Okla., 2017.

Smith, Martin, and Megan Brickley. *People of the Long Barrows: Life, Death and Burial in the Earlier Neolithic.* Stroud, UK: The History Press, 2009.

Snook, Jim. *Ice Age Extinction: Cause and Human Consequences.* New York: Algora Publishing, 2007.

Soni, Priyanka, et al. "Pharmacological Properties of *Datura stramonium L.* as a Potential Medicinal Tree: An Overview." *Asian Pacific Journal of Tropical Biomedicine* 2 (2012).

Sparks, Rachel Thyrza, Bill Finlayson, Bart Wagemakers, and Josef Mario Briffa, eds. *Digging up Jericho: Past, Present and Future.* Oxford, UK: Archaeopress, 2020.

Spencer, A. Jeffrey. *Early Egypt: The Rise of Civilization in the Nile Valley.* London: British Museum Press, 1993.

Spier, Leslie, Alfred L. Kroeber, and Robert Lowie. *Klamath Ethnography.* Berkeley: University of California Press, 1930.

Stanley, D. J. *Geological Evolution of the Mediterranean Basin.* New York: Springer, 1985.

Stanley, D. J. "Nile Silt Yields Secret of Egyptian Civilization." *New Scientist* 1883 (1993).

Steele, John. *Ocean Currents.* Cambridge, Mass.: Academic Press, 2009.

Stilborg, Ole. "Regionality in the Study of the Ertebolle Culture." *Archaeological Dialogues* 6 (1999).

Stout, Geraldine, and Matthew Stout. *Newgrange*. Cork, Ireland: Cork University Press, 2008.

Strong, Gordon. *Stanton Drew and Its Ancient Stone Circles*. London: Bloomsbury, 2009.

Suh, Anna, ed. *Leonardo's Notebooks: Writing and Art of the Great Master*. New York: Black Dog & Leventhal, 2013.

Tacitus. *The Agricola and the Germania*. Translated by B. Mattingly and J. B. Rivers. London: Penguin, 2010.

Tedlock, Dennis. *Popol Vuh: The Definitive Edition of the Mayan Book of the Dawn of Life and the Glories of Gods and Kings*. New York: Simon & Schuster, 1996.

Thom, Alexander. *Megalithic Remains in Britain and Brittany*. Oxford, UK: Oxford University Press, 1978.

Thomas, Julian. *The Birth of Neolithic Britain: An Interpretive Account*. Oxford, UK: Oxford University Press, 2013.

Thomas, Julian. *Understanding the Neolithic*. Abingdon, UK: Routledge, 2002.

Tilley, Christopher. *An Ethnography of the Neolithic: Early Prehistoric Societies in Southern Scandinavia*. Cambridge, UK: Cambridge University Press, 2008.

Toghill, Peter. *Geology of Britain—An Introduction*. London: Airlife Publishing, 2000.

Turner, Val. *Ancient Shetland*. London: Batsford, 1998.

Underwood, Peter. *Where the Ghosts Walk: The Gazetteer of Haunted Britain*. London: Souvenir Press, 2013.

Vail, Gabrielle, and Anthony Aveni, eds. *Madrid Codex: New Approaches to Understanding an Ancient Maya Manuscript*. Boulder: University Press of Colorado, 2004.

Voorhies, Barbara, and Douglas Kennett. "Buried Sites on the Soconusco Coastal Plain, Chiapas, Mexico." *Journal of Field Archaeology* 22 no. 1. (1995).

Wainwright, Geoffrey J. *Durrington Walls: Excavations 1966–1968*. London: The Society of Antiquaries, 1971.

Watkins, Alfred. *The Old Straight Track*. London: Sphere, 1974.

Weir, Anthony. *Early Ireland: A Field Guide*. Belfast, UK: Blackstaff Press, 1980.

Whittle, Alasdair. *Europe in the Neolithic: The Creation of New Worlds*. Cambridge, UK: Cambridge University Press, 2010.

Wickham-Jones, C.R. S. Dawson, and R. Bates. "Drowned Stone Age Settlement of the Bay of Firth, Orkney, Scotland." Report for the Waitt Foundation, La Jolla, Calif., 2010.

Wickham-Jones, Caroline. *Monuments of Orkney*. Edinburgh, UK: Historic Scotland, 2015.

Wickham-Jones, Caroline. *Orkney: A Historical Guide*. Edinburgh, UK: Birlinn, 2015.

Wilkinson, Toby. *The Rise and Fall of Ancient Egypt*. London: Bloomsbury, 2011.

Williams, S. "Skimming the Surface of Underwater Landslides." *Proceedings of the National Academy of Sciences of the United States of America* 113 (2016).

Wylie, Jonathan. *The Faroe Islands: Interpretations of History*. Lexington: The University Press of Kentucky, 2021.

Yang, Lihui, et al. *Handbook of Chinese Mythology*. Oxford, UK: Oxford University Press, 2008.

Yoffee, N., and J. J. Clark, eds. *Early stages in the evolution of Mesopotamian civilization*. Tucson: University of Arizona Press, 1993.

Index

Numbers in *italics* preceded by *pl.* refer to color insert plate numbers.